A Short History of San Diego

D1283588

For my beloved Sara, without whom none of this would mean anything, for Sissy who tries so hard to be good to me and for Penny Lee and Bryan who have gone on ahead and wait for us all.

And a brief acknowledgement to someone without whom this book probably would have never been started: To Desa Belyea, newspaper editor, who one day found a person wandering around in her city room and took a very big chance by having him write things for her.

A Short History of San Diego

Michael McKeever

San Francisco

First published in 1985 by
Lexikos
San Francisco, California

Project Direction: Robin Kirk
Designed by Craig Bergquist
Production by Carlton Herrick
Text set in Stempel Palatino by Heyday Books

Copyright © Michael McKeever 1985

All rights reserved. No part of this book may be
used or reproduced in any manner whatsoever
except for brief quotations embodied in critical
articles and reviews.

Manufactured in the United States of America.

Library of Congress Cataloging in Publication
Data:

McKeever, Michael
    A short history of San Diego.

    Bibliography: p.
    Includes index.
    1. San Diego (Calif.)—History. I. Title.
F869.S22M36 1985   979.4'98   84–40743
ISBN 0–938530–32–1
      86 87 5 4 3 2

Contents

Footprints in the Sand

1

Embedded in the brown earth of a bluff near the seaside community of Del Mar, the pale bone might have been mistaken for one of the stones surrounding it. But Malcolm Rogers of the San Diego Museum of Man recognized it as something very different. Carefully he released it from the earth. It was an old skull, soon dubbed "Del Mar Man."

No one could be certain in that year of 1929 just how old it was. But Rogers and the museum staff figured it had to be prehistoric, because its shape resembled prehistoric skulls found in other parts of the world.

In 1974, Del Mar Man was scientifically dated for the first time. Dr. Jeffrey Bada of the Scripps Institution of Oceanography used a dating technique based on amino acids and found that Del Mar Man was about forty-eight thousand years old. Recent studies strongly dispute this age, but it is at least certain that the mysterious Del Mar Man walked these shores long before the Indians were encountered by the Spanish.

A few miles south of Del Mar, the bones of another Indian people have been found beneath the wealthy suburb of La Jolla. These people, called the "La Jollans," were shell gatherers who lived here six thousand years ago. Today, they would still recognize these largely unchanged beaches, where they once searched for food in the rocks and tide pools.

"When Red Cane [the white man] comes We Wintu forget our songs Down West Down West we dance We spirits dance We spirits weeping dance."
—song of the Northern California Wintu

The Kumeyaay Presence: Around 1000 B.C., the La Jollans were confronted by a desert people from Arizona. The newcomers were called the Kumeyaay, and they spoke a Hokan language related to the tongue of the Yumas and Mojaves of the Colorado River. The Kumeyaay eventually dominated the La Jollans, who vanished from the land. It is not known

Opposite page

Ceremonies: This early 18th century French watercolor shows California Indians in "costumes of dance and war."

Arms and Utensils: Expertly crafted though they were, the California Indians' handiworks were not gold.

The La Jolla Beach and Tennis Club stands on a once-fertile archaeological site. Before the beach was developed and the freshwater lagoon filled in, several skeletons from the early La Jollan culture were found there.

precisely what happened to them, but it has been suggested that they were pushed south to become the primitive tribes of Baja California reported by Spanish missionaries.

Marks of the Kumeyaay presence can still be seen today. Stone grinding bowls called *metates* that were used for grinding acorns are occasionally found hidden in the grass beneath oak trees. Chipped-stone tools have been found in the marshes at the southern tip of San Diego Bay. Beneath a former drive-in theater in Pacific Beach, archaeologists have found broken bits of pottery from Kumeyaay tribes who spent the winter by the sea.

The Kumeyaay were a migratory people, moving with the seasons. In the warmth of summer, they might stay near the coast to catch the birds and fish of the marshes or to gather shellfish along the shore. Or they might move into the Cuyamaca Mountains to hunt deer and rabbits and gather acorns from tribal groves. They planted no seeds but instead harvested what the earth offered. At least sixty wild plants have been identified as food sources of the Kumeyaay. With winter, they would stop the wandering hunt for food and settle into permanent villages. Called *rancherías* by the Spanish, these villages were numerous; eight sites have been found around San Diego Bay alone.

Though largely untroubled by ambition and greed, Kumeyaay bands sometimes clashed in battle. But unlike the Sioux and Cheyenne of the plains, they never raised warfare to a fine art. Instead, their fighting was swift and brutal, often sparked by a quarrel over land. They would meet in battle with bows and arrows and wooden war clubs. Warriors would whirl and dance around camp fires at night, displaying bloody scalps and boasting of their bravery.

Living in a warm land, the Kumeyaay wore little. When the winter nights grew chill, they might drape a cloak of rabbit skins across their shoulders. To protect their feet from hot sand and nettles, they wore sandals of yucca fiber. Women used a woven apron-like garment; men and women alike decorated their faces by painful tattooing done with cactus spines and charcoal.

Speaking a babel of dialects, they were sometimes prisoners of their own language, unable to communicate even with neighboring tribes. Friar Geronimo Boscanna, of the Mission San Juan Capistrano, wrote: "The diversity of language is so great... that almost every 15 or 20 leagues, you find a distinct dialect; so different, that in no way does one resemble the other... The natives of San Diego cannot understand a word of the language used in this mission, and in like manner, those in the neighborhood of Santa Barbara, and farther north."

Corridor of Time: Malcolm Rogers (foreground) and E. Hardy inspect a northern San Diego County excavation in 1938.

Dance of Mourning: To the Kumeyaay, the passage of time and the life of the community were marked by ceremonies. Richard F. Pourade describes their rituals in his exemplary work, *The Explorers*:

Girls were forced to swallow balls of tobacco. Later they were placed on their backs in pits lined with heated stones, and then more warmed flat stones were placed on their abdomens. Here they remained for three days... In turn, boys in their final ceremony were laid on anthills, or put into a hole containing ants, and then more insects were shaken over them from baskets. It... was concluded when the ants were whipped from their bodies with stinging nettles.

Kumeyaay dead were cremated and a dance of mourning was performed to the sound of reed flutes and rattles made of deer hooves. The Kumeyaay gathered around campfires at night to hear a rich mythology of gods and men, told by the older people who understood the spirits.

Today, many of the old ways of San Diego's Indians have been lost. The strong nets, the pottery, and the baskets so wonderfully made that they could hold water are among the Kumeyaay's lost arts. In the aftermath of the Spanish and American settlements, the Indians had their songs and their stories—their very way of life—taken from them. Even the names of their tribes and clans have been largely replaced by names taken from the Spanish missions around which they eventually clustered—Diegueños near Mission San Diego and Luiseños near Mission San Luis Rey. So it was that, even as the Wintu of northern California sang their own lament, the Kumeyaay of San Diego saw their ancient culture passing into memory.

Basketweaver: Bunch grass with which the Kumeyaay once weaved baskets has largely disappeared. However, in the mountains at Cuyamaca Rancho State Park, large stands of bunch grass still survive.

Men in Armor: In 1542, a world away in Europe, the Renaissance was faltering in a series of savage wars. On San Diego Bay, the peace of centuries was nearing its end. Soon the world of the Kumeyaay would disappear in a whirlwind of change.

On September 28, 1542, men unlike any seen before by the Kumeyaay stepped ashore at San Diego Bay. To the wonder of the Indians, the strangers were bearded. Their bodies were encased in metal armor, and they wore leather boots and carried swords and guns. Their ships, the *San Salvador* and the *La Victoria*, rolled on the swells of the bay. High above the sterns floated the gold and scarlet flag of imperial Spain.

The Spaniards, led by Juan Rodríguez Cabrillo, were both explorers and dreamers, searching for fabulous cities and mythical sea passages. To them, the Indians were a disappointment; their way of life offered no gold or jewels.

Cabrillo wrote in his journal that the Indians were fearful: "Three of [the Kumeyaay] waited but all the rest fled . . . They gave signs of great fear. On the night of this day, our men went ashore from the ships to fish with a net, and it appears that here there were some Indians, and they began to shoot at them with arrows and wounded three men."

The Indians had reason to be afraid. From desert tribes to the east, news of the terror and death brought by other Spanish explorers had passed from one Indian to another.

Cabrillo continued in his journal:

Indians came to the ships and said by signs that in the interior, men like us were travelling about, bearded, clothed and armed like those of the ships. They made signs that they carried crossbows and swords; and they made gestures with the right arm as if they were throwing lances and ran around as if they were on horseback. They made signs that they [Spaniards] were killing many Indians, and that for this reason they were afraid.

After resting in the sheltered bay for seven days, the Spaniards raised anchor and set sail northward. It would be a century and a half before another Spanish ship anchored in the bay. With the days of conquest at an end, this ship would come in search of safe harbors for trading vessels. By that time, Cabrillo's visit had faded from the campfire stories of the Kumeyaay.

Today, the Kumeyaay legacy is found in the pages of archaeologists' notebooks, in museum exhibits of arrowheads and empty baskets once filled with acorn meal, and in the traditions carried in the memories of those who live on the scattered reservations of San Diego County.

The actual location of the Spanish landing is a matter of conjecture since nature and man have changed the shoreline throughout the years. Historians believe that Cabrillo anchored just inside Ballast Point, one mile inside the bay, and sent his ship's small boat to explore.

Today in San Diego County, about 7500 Indians live in cities and towns, while 2500 are scattered on 17 reservations throughout the backcountry.

Gilded Dreams

2

In the Portugal of his birth, his name was spelled João Rodrigues Cabrilho. But to the Spanish whom he served, he was Juan Rodríguez Cabrillo. In late 1542, as his ships, the *San Salvador* and the *La Victoria*, neared the coast of what is now southern California, Cabrillo had already sailed farther north than any other captain. He was among the last of his breed.

Many others had come before him. For a half century, Spain's soldiers and sailors had pushed deeper into the unknown New World. Christopher Columbus was the first to strike out for the New World, sailing in 1492. After he had returned to the court of Ferdinand and Isabella, he crossed the Atlantic again on three more voyages of discovery. Soon, sailors' tales were being told in the waterfront taverns of Spain and Portugal.

Beyond the western seas, they claimed, was a new land with a river so vast and powerful that, far from land, a man could dip his cup into the ocean and taste sweet water. The river banks were guarded by women warriors like the Amazons of mythology. There were many such stories; the most tantalizing were tales of jungle cities whose golden towers gleamed in the sun.

With each new discovery, the tales grew wilder, the reality more grim. By 1521, scarcely three decades after Columbus first touched the new shores, the powerful Aztec military empire had been destroyed by Hernán Cortés and his conquistadors. By 1532, the Inca empire had been seized and the Inca lord brutally murdered by Francisco Pizarro and his men.

The Northern Mystery: Her treasury swollen with gold looted from the Aztec and Inca empires, Spain turned her attention northward. Her maps ended in the barren stretches of northern Mexico—the land

Opposite page
Intruders: To the Indians, the European ships were first a benign novelty, then an instrument of their decline.

Tales of fabulous golden cities held an enduring fascination for the Spanish. One popular fable told of the lost Kingdom of La Gran Quivira, where gold was so common it was used to make pots and pans.

beyond was a mystery. Many had theories, but some were so certain of what they would find that they had already chosen a name—California.

They took it from a book, *Las Sergas de Esplandian*, by Garcí Ordóñez de Montalvo, a Spanish writer of whimsical tales. Montalvo wrote of an island "rich beyond all dreams lying at the right hand of the Indies" and "very close to the Terrestrial Paradise." Named for its beautiful virgin queen Calafia, it "is known to all its people as 'California.'"

But there was another, more pressing reason for Spain to probe the north—the search for the Strait of Anian. There was a theory that, above Mexico, a great sea passage linking the Atlantic and Pacific Oceans would be found. Should such a passage be discovered, Spain's galleons could sail to both her Atlantic and Pacific ports with ease. As it was, the ships' crews were forced to off-load their cargo in Panamanian ports, caravan by pack mule from sea to sea through the jungles of the isthmus, and reload the cargo onto other ships. With the discovery of the Strait of Anian, not only would Spain's Pacific ports prosper, but her treasure galleons would have an easy route to the wealth of the Orient.

A **Hellish Voyage:** In 1532, eleven years after the fall of the Aztec citadel of Tenochtitlán, the aging conquistador Cortés sent two small ships from the western Mexican port of Zacatula to begin probing the unknown area north of Mexico. The expedition ended abruptly in a shipwreck on the eastern beaches of the Gulf of California.

Cortés sent two more ships a year later. The historical documents describe a hellish voyage. The first night out, the crew of one ship were startled to find themselves alone on the sea. They had been deserted by the captain of the second ship, who had sailed off in search of his own glory, eventually discovering the Revilla Gigedo Islands 420 miles off the Mexican coast.

The remaining ship sailed on, buffeted by storms. The crew began to plot against their captain, a tyrant named Diego de Becerra. One night, the ship's pilot murdered the sleeping Becerra and took command. Eventually, the ship anchored in a bay the Spanish named Santa Cruz, now known as the Mexican resort city of La Paz in lower Baja California.

When the men went ashore, they were ambushed by Indians, and 21 Spaniards were killed. The survivors abandoned the ship at anchor and made a desperate voyage in the ship's boat to the mainland. There they fell into the hands of one Nuño de Guzmán, a political enemy of Cortés.

Guzmán was powerful and wealthy, his fortune built on the buying and selling of slaves. In 1530, to curb the growing power of the conquistadors in the

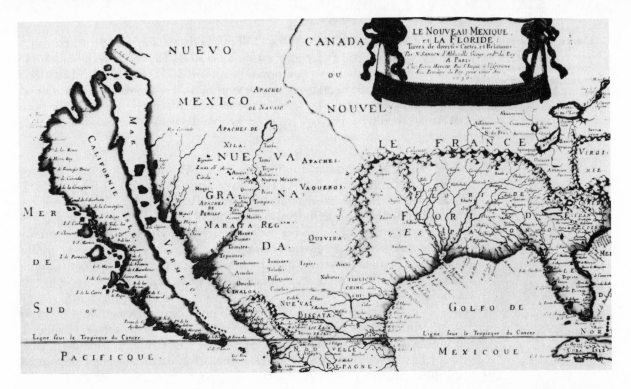

New World, the Spanish crown had set up a system of administrative courts. Guzmán was the first judge appointed. He imprisoned the wretched survivors, who sat in their cells babbling about the oyster beds of Santa Cruz and the gleaming pearls waiting to be plucked from the bottom of the bay.

When the news of his men's imprisonment reached him, Cortés appealed to a second *audencia*. That court refused to overturn Guzmán's decision and instead ordered Cortés to cease further exploration. But Cortés was intrigued by the pearls. He ignored the court's order and determined to make the next voyage himself.

In describing the Indians of Santa Cruz, historians have used words like "savage," "hostile" and "primitive." And, as Ralph Roske wrote in his history of California, *Everyman's Eden*, the Indians "proved to be totally uninterested in diving for [pearls for] the Europeans. Consequently, Cortés had to be content with the shells torn loose and tossed on the beach." In the end, the venture was a failure, producing only poverty, starvation, and the death of 23 men.

In 1535, Cortés sent out yet another expedition of three ships under the command of Francisco de Ulloa. Ulloa intended to sail around Baja California, which the Spanish were certain was an island, and perhaps find the elusive

Century-old Mistake: More than 100 years after the Spanish had proved otherwise, French mapmakers persisted in showing California as an island.

When Cabrillo sailed in 1542, the Ottoman Turks had just taken Hungary, the Scots and the English were at war, and France took up arms when a German king made his son the ruler of an Italian state.

Strait of Anian. He sailed up the Gulf of California, known to the Spanish as the Vermillion Sea, as far as the Colorado River Delta. There he unhappily revised his charts. Lower California, he reported, was not an island at all, but only the peninsula of an even greater land mass. Frustrated and disillusioned, Ulloa began the voyage back down the Mexican coast. The search for the Strait of Anian would have to be carried on by someone else.

The Last Conquistador: Juan Rodríguez Cabrillo had fought in the ranks of Cortés in the Valley of Mexico at the terrible siege of Tenochtitlán in 1521. He was there when Guatemóc, last of the Aztec warrior-princes, humbled himself before the Spaniards. Bernal Díaz del Castillo, who was also there, later wrote: "I remember the man . . . Juan Rodríguez Cabrillo, who was a good soldier in the Mexican campaign . . . He served His Majesty well in everything which presented itself to him." After the battle for Mexico, Cabrillo left the forces of Cortés and moved south with Pedro de Alvarado to take Guatemala.

Cabrillo, among the last of the original conquistadors, was living in semiretirement in Guatemala in 1536. When the governor of Guatemala announced plans to build ships to explore the Pacific and the unknown coasts to the north, Cabrillo could not resist a final adventure. He set up a shipyard at the little Guatemalan port of Iztapa and began building ships for the great exploration.

Cabrillo sailed from Guatemala in June of 1542, while in Europe the armies of a dozen nations and city-states pushed each other across the continent. To him, the wars were far away and meaningless. His expedition in the *San Salvador* and *La Victoria* would be one of the last voyages into the map's blank spaces. Those after him would plot their voyages on the charts that Cabrillo left as his legacy.

On September 26, 1542, after two months at sea, Cabrillo's crew saw the Coronado Islands. The sighting was duly noted in the expedition log: "They sailed along the coast about eight leagues, passing by some three islands completely denuded of soil. One of them is larger than the others. They are three leagues from the mainland. They called them the 'Desert Islands.'"

Two days later, Cabrillo's ships glided past Point Loma into San Diego Bay. The crew stayed six days. They were pleased with the harbor, calling it "closed and very good." Prayers were offered and the proper ceremonies completed. The port was entered onto the charts as San Miguel and deemed a possible haven for Spain's ships. An entry in the expedition journal reads: "While . . . in this port a heavy storm occurred, but since the port is good, they did not feel it at all. It was a violent storm from the west-southwest."

On the seventh day, they sailed northward out of the harbor. To the Kumeyaay, their visit would become part of the camp fire tales.

Not long afterward, on what is now San Miguel Island north of Santa Catalina, Cabrillo fell and was injured. Infection set in, and he died at sea two months later. Returning to San Miguel, his grieving officers and men buried their captain.

A mournful entry was made in the log: "Passing the Winter on the Island of La Posesión, on the third of the month of January, 1543, Juan Rodríguez Cabrillo departed from this life, as the result of a fall which he suffered on said island when they were there before." He left the chief pilot, Bartolomé Ferrelo, as captain. At the time of his death, Cabrillo emphatically charged his crew "not to leave off exploring as much as possible of all that coast."

With Ferrelo in command, the expedition turned northward again. Eventually, they found themselves off the forested coast of southern Oregon. There, tossed by storms and with dwindling supplies, they turned about and started home.

Cabrillo holds an honored place in our history. At San Diego's Cabrillo National Monument at Point Loma, a statue of the explorer carved by Portugal's Alvaro deBree watches boldly over the harbor he first entered so long ago. At San Miguel's Cuyler Harbor, a stone cross has been erected in his memory.

"This day great smokes were seen on the land. The country appears to be good and has large valleys. And in the interior there are high mountains."
—Cabrillo's expedition log, September 27, 1542

Lighthouse: First lighted in 1855, the old San Diego Lighthouse is Cabrillo National Monument's principal historic structure.

Gravestone: The absence of a C on the gravestone thought to be Cabrillo's can be easily explained. Cabrillo was known to his men, and signed his name, as Juan Rodriguez. He rarely used his surname.

Cabrillo's Gravestone: No one is certain where Cabrillo's grave lies on San Miguel. Recently, the mystery of the grave site has deepened. In 1901, a strange slab of stone with cryptic markings was found on Santa Rosa Island, located next to San Miguel. Removed to the University of California at Berkeley, the stone sat on a dusty shelf in a back room of the Lowie Museum until 1972, when Dr. Robert Heizer became intrigued by the mysterious markings.

The stone is gray, about 14 inches long, 4 inches wide, and 3 inches thick. In the upper left corner is a cross, and below, the letters J and R are joined together. On the bottom of the slab is a crude stick figure of a man.

This strange stone may be Cabrillo's grave marker. It conforms to the style of many other gravestones of the period, and there is some linguistic evidence that the island Cabrillo called La Posesión was in reality Santa Rosa and not San Miguel. It has also been suggested that Indians might have removed the stone from the grave and carried it off. Perhaps an Indian carved the stick figure on the base, which is not typical of such Spanish grave markers.

Heizer and other experts believe that the stone is not a hoax, but warn that it still cannot be proved to be Cabrillo's grave marker. Since it was found unattached to any grave, the actual burial site of the famed conquistador remains a mystery. The debate will probably continue until, as Heizer points out, either the grave or Cabrillo's journal is found. Meanwhile, the stone remains in the Lowie Museum in Berkeley (a replica is on exhibit at the Cabrillo National Monument).

Treasure of the Land: Ironically, when the Cabrillo expedition returned to Mexico, Spanish officials were disappointed. The explorers had found neither treasure nor lost cities nor the Strait of Anian. The many nautical charts that showed soundings and safe anchorages were simply cataloged and stored away.

Cabrillo's enemies chipped away at his land and wealth until his widow was reduced to poverty. In time, she remarried, but the bitterness continued for many years. Investigations were conducted for decades, as Cabrillo's descendants continued to plead for the restoration of the family wealth. Eventually, even the conquistador's great-great-grandchildren entered claims.

Had San Diego been a land of obvious wealth, Spanish officials might have been more impressed with Cabrillo's discovery, and more sympathetic to his family's claims. But the treasure of this land was of a nature unappreciated by the bureaucracy. Not until many years later, amid tangled court intrigues, would the fate of San Diego again be considered. Then the charts of Cabrillo would be brought out and unrolled once more.

With Cross and Sword

3

In March, 1596, three small ships raised anchor on the west coast of Mexico and beat their way northwest towards Baja California. The leader of the expedition, Sebastián Vizcaíno, had scrounged his crew from the waterfronts of the New World. His destination was Santa Cruz, where he intended to found a colony.

The Spain Vizcaíno served was far different from the Spain of the conquistadors. In the eight years since the defeat of her great Armada off the coast of England, Spain's power had diminished dramatically. Now, the king's tax collectors increasingly took their due from commerce rather than conquest, and that commerce needed protection.

The Manila galleons were an important part of Spain's trading economy. These huge treasure ships, filled with wealth from the Orient, crossed the Pacific from Manila to Acapulco. Despite their imposing appearance, the galleons were fragile and vulnerable. In the beginning, they had sailed alone, safe on what the Spanish thought of as their "lake," the Pacific Ocean. But in 1575, English warships prowled the Pacific, tracking down and capturing the fat, slow galleons. As English captain Thomas Cavendish boasted in 1587 after capturing the galleon *Santa Ana*, "I made great spoils: I burnt and sank nine ships, small and great . . . I had taken great quantities of treasure."

An even more audacious English captain was Sir Francis Drake who, after looting his way from Peru to California, landed north of San Francisco Bay in June, 1579. There, he claimed what he called Nova Albion for Queen Elizabeth. After repairing his ship, the *Golden Hind*, he returned to England. He left behind " . . . a plate of brasse, fast nailed to a great and firm poste, whereon is engraved her grace's name and 16th day and year of our arivall there, and of the free giving up of the province and kingdome, both by the king and the people, into Her Majestie's hands."

The first Englishman to raid the galleons was John Oxenham who, in late 1575 stunned the Spanish by taking two galleons with a jerry-built boat. Though Oxenham was later captured and hung, the secret was out: Spanish treasure could be taken with ease.

Opposite page
The Brown Robes: California's Franciscan missionaries were zealous and dedicated, sometimes tragically so.

Drake's name for California
—Nova Albion—was used
35 years later by John Smith
when he mapped New
England.

With the English loose in the Pacific, Spain became concerned about the vulnerable west coast of Mexico. Coastal settlements with safe harbors were clearly necessary, and Santa Cruz seemed a good beginning.

Vizcaíno was not the most popular choice to lead the expedition. As the Conde de Monterey, Viceroy of Mexico, wrote, "Vizcaíno's quality and capital are not sufficient in connection with an enterprise which may come to be of such vast importance." As later events would prove, the Viceroy was a good judge of character. But for the time being, Vizcaíno prevailed, and the expedition set sail with the Viceroy's tepid blessings.

Vizcaíno's problems began even before he reached Baja California. There were desertions at each anchorage along the Mexican coast. When the three ships turned northwest to cross the Gulf of California, his ranks were thinner by fifty men. Arriving at Santa Cruz in mid-1596, Vizcaíno renamed it La Paz, by which name we know it today. The Spanish soon got into a squabble with the Indians. Shots were fired and several Indians were killed. The Spaniards fled in small boats, but an Indian arrow wounded a man, panic ensued, and a boat capsized, drowning 19 men.

Disaster piled on disaster. In October, 1596, the tattered collection of would-be empire builders sailed home to Mexico. Behind them, the milky-white pearls of La Paz remained as elusive as ever.

Despite his failure at La Paz, Vizcaíno, a masterful self-promoter, was given another chance. In May, 1602, he set sail along the western coast of California in three small ships. This time, however, he sailed with a firm set of instructions, one of which was to locate safe anchorages for the Manila galleons.

San Diego Rediscovered: On November 10, 1602, the ships dropped anchor in the sweeping, silent bay Cabrillo had called San Miguel. Vizcaíno had been told not to rename earlier discoveries, but he was unable to restrain himself. November 12 marked the feast day of San Diego de Alcalá, whom Pope Sixtus V had proclaimed a saint 14 years before. The charts were rolled out, and a new name scratched in place of Cabrillo's San Miguel. The name was now San Diego.

Like Cabrillo, Vizcaíno was impressed with the bay. Father Antonio de la Asención wrote in the expedition journal that San Diego was "a port which must be the best to be found in all the South Sea . . . being protected on all sides and having good anchorage. It has very good wood and water and many fish of all kinds. On the land there is much game."

After resting four days, Vizcaíno continued up the California coast. A month later he put into a wind-blown bay surrounded by fog-shrouded forests,

Adarga —2 layer rawhide shield. Design outlined by rawhide stitching.

A Cuera [spanish dragoon]

La Espada [sword]

carabina [carbine]

Soldados de Cuero: **Leather-jacketed soldiers were the last vanguard of Spanish imperialism.**

hundreds of miles to the north of San Diego. With considerable license, Vizcaíno reported that he had found "the best port that could be desired, for besides being sheltered from all the winds, it has many pines for masts and yards . . . and water in great quantity, all near the shore." With a dash of diplomacy, he named it Monterey Bay in honor of the Viceroy. More than 150 years after Vizcaíno had wandered into the mists of history, explorers were still searching for his wonderful bay. In 1769, Gaspar de Portolá actually stood on its shores. But, relying upon Vizcaíno's exaggerated description, Portolá failed to recognize it and went off to continue his search.

Great Plans: San Diego was unvisited for a century and a half following Vizcaíno's rediscovery. By 1768, Spain had become a weak giant, bled by war and decay. It had made virtually no progress in colonizing the lands north of Mexico. But other, more robust powers were on the prowl. The English had consumed most of the eastern half of North America. The Royal Navy patrolled from the ice floes of the Canadian north to the tip of Florida, and with its island bases in the Caribbean, England was growing uncomfortably close to Spain's holdings in the New World. Another threat loomed on the Pacific coast—the Russians had reached across from Siberia to take Alaska, and were edging down toward Spanish California.

Spain no longer looked to dreamers and warriors to hold her North American empire. Instead, she would garrison her frontier outposts with common soldiers, carpenters, ranchers, and priests, many of them born in the colonies. The time of practicality was at hand.

In 1768, a plan to settle California was prepared under the direction of José de Gálvez, Inspector General of New Spain, and the Spanish king's representative in Mexico. Carefully conceived and written, Gálvez' plan looked good. The first move north would come in five land and sea waves, each with San Diego as its destination. There they would rejoin and start a settlement. Soon after, a column would set out for the Monterey of Vizcaíno's description. On arrival at Monterey, a garrison would be established to blunt the Russian threat from the north. The entire effort, called the Sacred Expedition, was placed in the experienced hand of Captain Gaspar de Portolá.

In March, 1769, the first of the expedition's columns moved out from the Baja California mission of Velicatá under the command of a tough, efficient soldier, Captain Fernando de Rivera y Moncada. Protecting Moncada's string of 180 pack mules rode a platoon of twenty-five *soldados de cuero* (leather jacket soldiers). Two months later, a second column left the Baja California mission of Santa María led by Portolá. Riding on a borrowed army mule was a fifty-five-year-old Franciscan priest, known for his sharp tongue and a fondness for chocolate. His name was Junípero Serra.

Serra's poultice was the same used by muleskinners for animal sores.

Although he was president of the Missions, Serra had been discouraged from going on the expedition because of a badly infected leg. Father Francisco Palóu had asked to go in his place, later writing, "When I saw the wound and the swelling of his foot and leg, I could not restrain my tears, when I considered how much he would have to suffer traveling over the arduous roads known to exist up to the frontier, as well as those still unknown and later to be found, with no other physician and surgeon with him but the Divine Healer."

But Serra would not be put off. "Let us not speak of that. I have placed all of my confidence in God, of whose goodness I hope that He will grant me to reach not only San Diego, but also Monterey." Along the way, Serra treated himself with a poultice of mud and herbs and, by the time the column reached San Diego, the leg was much better.

Founder of the Missions: Junípero Serra's Franciscans founded 21 missions along California's Camino Real.

The **Wished-for Harbor:** Even as the land columns made their way north through the deserts of Baja California, the other three fingers of the Sacred Expedition were underway by sea. In early January, 1769, the ship *San Carlos* sailed under Royal Navy Captain Vicente Vila. A month and a half later, the *San Antonio*, commanded by Juan Pérez, followed. Finally, in June, the heavily-laden supply ship *San Jose* rounded Cape San Lucas on her way to San Diego.

On April 11, 1769, the *San Antonio* dropped anchor in the protective arm of Point Loma's Ballast Point. Eighteen days later, the overdue *San Carlos* entered San Diego Bay and anchored near the *San Antonio*. Following Vizcaíno's clumsy maps, she had lost her way. Scurvy had ravaged the crew, and the ship's log listed the mounting toll. "On April 18-19: At one o'clock in the afternoon, Fernando Alvarez, the boatswain's second mate and coxswain of the launch, died . . . April 23-24: On this day the sick . . . confessed and received the sacrament. At six o'clock in the evening Manuel Reyes [the pilot] died . . . at eight in the morning, the body of Reyes was cast overboard."

Taken ashore, the *San Carlos'* men continued to sicken and die, along with several from the *San Antonio*. Expedition surgeon Pedro Prat scoured the shoreline for green plants to combat the scurvy. But for many of the sailors, help came too late.

It has been estimated that of the 159 people who arrived at San Diego approximately 60 eventually died of scurvy. When the *San Antonio* returned south with expedition reports in July, 1769, she mustered a crew of eight men. On her arrival at San Blas, only two sailors were left alive.

The two ships huddled together in the great empty bay and waited for the expedition's third ship, the *San Jose*. She had left La Paz filled with church bells and bronze cannon for a fortress, and was noisy with crates of squawking chickens—but she was never seen again.

In mid-May, Moncada arrived with his leather-jacketed soldiers. They stood on a mesa overlooking what is now the estuary of the Tia Juana River and the town of Imperial Beach. A priest in the column, Father Juan Crespí, wrote, "From a little height on this plain, we made out that the sea ran far inland; and in it we caught sight of the ships' mainmasts, scarcely visible from the distance they were at. I do not know how to tell the happiness and joy we all felt at seeing the hour arrive of our reaching the long-wished-for harbor of San Diego."

Six weeks later, on the first of July, Portolá's column arrived. The Sacred Expedition, minus one ship and numerous casualties, was reunited. After a two-week rest, Portolá and a column of 74 soldiers, priests, and Christian Indians from Baja California, began the 600-mile march north to find Monterey (and, unexpectedly, San Francisco Bay).

Father Serra remained at San Diego. Like those who had come before him, he was pleased with what he found. "Thanks be to God, I arrived at this Port of San Diego. It is beautiful to behold and does not belie its reputation."

On the morning of July 16, 1769, on a scrubby hill overlooking what is now Old Town, Serra offered High Mass before a rough wooden cross. He gave a sermon, the words lost to us, but the men who listened knew that the cost in human life to reach that hill had been high. They could not know yet, but it would become higher.

On August 15th, the Kumeyaay Indians attacked the tiny settlement of reed huts and killed a young Spaniard named José María Vergerano. The soldiers drove the Indians back, killing five. The dead boy was buried and prayers said over his grave. Construction began on a defensive stockade. The Spanish had come to San Diego before. This time they meant to stay.

Outposts of Faith

4

In the summer of 1769, the struggling settlement at San Diego was wracked with sickness and hunger. Many men, weakened by scurvy, lay in makeshift cots while priests said the last rites over them. Of the 40 men left behind when Portolá struck out for Monterey, 19 men died before his return. Among the dead were six faithful Christian Indians who had followed the Spanish north from Baja California.

Famine awaited those who survived the sickness. Though a small garden was planted and a few stalks of corn harvested, it was not nearly enough. With ammunition in short supply, and the Kumeyaay bolder each day, hunting was curtailed. In the heat, the San Diego River began to disappear into the dry sand of the river bed.

Finding a reliable source of fresh water was a problem in San Diego's dry climate. Father Juan Crespí wrote in late May, "When we reached the port we found, about one league distant, a good river running with sufficient water; but in a few days it ran dry . . . We followed the course of the river. We found it dry in many places. In some spots there were pools with water, and in other places there was only a streamlet. We walked about three leagues up the river bed . . . when the bed narrowed, there was no running water."

The priests were further dismayed when the Kumeyaay resisted their gentle attempts at conversion. Father Francisco Palóu reported, "The missionaries tried by means of gifts and kind treatment to attract the pagans who presented themselves. But since these did not understand our language, they paid attention to nothing else but to accepting what was given them." At first, the Indians had been frightened by the Spanish, but the fear soon wore off. Father Palóu continued, "They were ignorant of the force of firearms and trusted in the strength of their numbers, as well as in their arrows and wooden

Opposite page
Colonial capital: Monterey's Presidio was for many years California's largest.

instruments, fashioned like sabers, which cut like steel. They also had instruments such as clubs or wooden mallets . . . So they began to rob without fear. They were willing to take a chance and by putting all of us to death they would take home the spoils."

Francisco Palóu: A typical missionary—zealous, tough, and far from home.

First Skirmish: Spanish losses would have been greater when the Indians made their first attack on August 15 if it hadn't been, as Father Palóu observed, that "When the Indians saw the soldiers putting on their leather jackets and defensive armor . . . and making ready their muskets, they started to flee and shot their arrows; meanwhile, the four soldiers, the carpenter and the blacksmith began to fire valiantly. The blacksmith especially, who doubtless was full of extraordinary spirit because he had just received Holy Communion . . . went in between the huts, shouting, 'Long live the Faith of Jesus Christ, and may these dogs, enemies of that faith, die!' At the same time he fired on the pagans." Five Kumeyaay warriors died in the attack. The Indians became less bold for a time.

The Kumeyaay, though subdued, continued to resist the new faith in the weeks following the attack. While they feared the soldiers, they mocked the missionaries. Francisco Palóu noted one particularly cruel joke which affected Serra deeply:

One evening the Kumeyaay even rafted out to the anchored *San Carlos* and attempted to steal a sail.

A pagan came . . . carrying in his arms a young child, and according to the signs he made he gave him to understand that he wanted it baptized. Our Venerable Father Serra was filled with joy and immediately brought forth some clothing to dress the child. He invited the corporal of the guard to act as godfather, and the other soldiers to attend and solemnize the first baptism, at which the Indians were also present. When the Venerable Father was finished with the preliminary ceremonies and just as he was about to pour the water, the pagans snatched the child and carried it away to their village, leaving the Venerable Father with the shell containing the baptismal water in his hand. At that moment he had to use all his prudence not to show resentment . . . and to restrain the soldiers from avenging the profanation. The grief of Our Venerable Father at being frustrated in baptizing was so great that it lasted for many days. When he would relate this incident, even many years later, he had to dry the tears running down his eyes.

It had been Serra's fondest hope to perform Alta California's first baptism, but on July 22, 1769, Fathers Gomez and Crespí baptized two dying Kumeyaay infants.

When Portolá's column returned from Monterey in January, 1770, the Kumeyaay's hostility was a growing source of concern. Expedition cartographer Miguel Costansó wrote, "There was every reason to fear the evil disposition of the natives of San Diego, whose greediness to rob can only be restrained by superior power and authority, and we feared lest they dared to commit some

Olive orchard: After thousands of years of hunting and gathering, California's Indians grew dependent on planned agriculture.

outrage against the mission and its small garrison."

Talk of Abandonment: Morale was low as Portolá and his men trudged into camp, smelling of the mules they had been forced to eat along the way. They had searched long and hard for Monterey Bay (and had even stood on its shore). But nothing had looked remotely like the wonderful bay of Vizcaíno's exaggerations.

On November 1, they halted on the southern shoreline of what Father Juan Crespí called a "great arm of the sea . . . which could not only contain all the navies of His Catholic Majesty, but those of all Europe as well." A scouting party under Sergeant José Ortega followed the edge of the huge bay north. Four days later, the scouts returned to report that a march of many miles would be required for the column to work its way around. Too worn to continue, Portolá gazed across the vast, still waters of what would soon be known as San Francisco Bay and gave the order to return to San Diego. Portolá reported to Serra that he had failed to find Monterey. The sharp-tongued priest snapped that Portolá had "come from Rome without having seen the Pope."

Portolá soon realized that without supplies the settlement could not hold on much longer. Several months before, the *San Antonio* had sailed south to

Spain's obsession with Vizcaíno's fantasies was so strong that the Empire long neglected far superior San Francisco Bay in favor of inferior Monterey.

bring back supplies, but hadn't returned. In February, Portolá sent a squad to the Baja California missions to try to pack in supplies. Finally, as his men grew weaker, he made the decision that if the supplies had not arrived by March 20, the settlement would be abandoned and the expedition would return to Mexico. A distraught Father Serra wrote, "There is even talk of abandonment and suppression of my poor little mission in San Diego. May God avert such a tragedy."

The patron saint of the expedition was St. Joseph, whose feast day was celebrated on March 19. On March 11, the missionaries began nine days of desperate prayer in a novena to him. On the final day, March 19, 1770, a high mass was sung in honor of "the glorious patriarch, St. Joseph." Throughout the morning, the Spaniards searched the horizon—there was only the empty sea. Then, at three o'clock in the afternoon, a shout was heard. Serra peered into the afternoon sun and saw a distant sail. It was the supply ship *San Antonio*. The priests' prayers had been answered; the "poor little mission" of San Diego would not be abandoned after all.

To the Spaniards' horror, the *San Antonio* sailed past San Diego towards Monterey (where it was expected that Portolá would be waiting). But off San Pedro an anchor was lost, so the captain returned to San Diego to borrow one off the *San Carlos*.

Relocating the Mission: As the colony took root and the first Indian converts trickled in, the priests faced a new problem. The garrison soldiers often treated the Kumeyaay harshly, cuffing the men about and displaying a brutal interest in the women. This behavior made the already difficult work of the missionaries even harder. In a report to the Viceroy of Mexico, Serra wrote:

> In the morning, six or more soldiers would set out together, with or without permission from the corporal, on horseback, and go to the far distant villages, even many leagues away. When both men and women at the sight of them took to their heels—and this account comes from the Fathers, who learned of it from the many declarations and complaints of the gentiles—the soldiers, clever as they are at lassoing cows and mules, would catch an Indian woman with their lassos to become prey for their unbridled lusts. At times some of the Indian men would try to defend their wives, only to be shot down by bullets... What with these occurrences and others, a year passed by, not only without making any serious progress, but more and more each day turning away the hearts of the gentiles, and pushing them farther away from where their true happiness lay.

Serra sought permission from the Viceroy to move the mission away from the garrison. In December, 1773, Julio Ramon Mendoza, Second Secretary to the Viceroy, authorized Serra to move the mission upriver, safe from "the bad influence of the military over the Mission Pueblo in its immediate vicinity."

A Short History of San Diego

In 1774, taking only a small guard, the priests left the hilltop presidio. They moved a few miles east along the San Diego River to a place they called Nuestra Señora del Pilar, near a large Kumeyaay village called Nipawi. There, from the mud, sticks, and reeds of the river, the priests and Christian Indians built a new mission.

Slowly, painfully, the colony grew into a stable community. Crops were coaxed from the reluctant soil and a few cattle began to dot the hillsides. More settlers arrived from Mexico; in early 1775, a settler's wife gave birth to a boy, the first Spanish child born in California.

Arrows in the Night: Meanwhile, in the Kumeyaay villages, there was growing resentment of the Spanish presence. The chiefs counseled for war and, in the cold pre-dawn of November 4, 1775, the warriors of 40 Kumeyaay villages gathered for battle.

They descended on the mission, their flaming arrows hissing and biting into the tinder-dry wooden buildings. At the cookhouse, the four soldiers of the mission guard piled bales of clothing in front of the door and opened fire. Two frightened boys, the nephew and son of the presidio commandant, huddled inside. Nearby, a mission carpenter, struck down in the first minutes of the attack, lay dying. Two of the soldiers at the cookhouse were wounded within moments. Eight feet in front of the stronghold, seen by the flickering light of the burning compound, lay a dead Kumeyaay warrior. The Indians hurled clubs, rocks, even chunks of burning wood in their fury.

The embattled soldiers heard the sound of gunfire from the blacksmith shop where two cornered blacksmiths and a priest fought for their lives. One smith, José Arroyo, died there, and the other, Felipe Romero, broke from the flames and ran to the cookhouse. Suddenly, gentle Father Luis Jayme, who refused to believe his beloved Indians would hurt him, ran toward them. His arms spread wide, he cried his familiar greeting, "Love God, my children!"

Father Jayme had been warned before not to be too trusting of the Indians, and Father Pedro Font later wrote that Jayme was convinced "it would be impossible that his Indians would do such a thing to him because he loved them greatly and favored them in every way he could."

The Indians seized Father Jayme and dragged him to the river. There, the Kumeyaay did their work. After the attack, he was found in the mud of the river bank, his body broken and barely recognizable. "The Indians," wrote Father Palóu bitterly, "realized he was a priest, and as wolves do to a young lamb, they laid hold of him, while he bore himself as one mute, not opening his lips."

Warrior: The Kumeyaay's few attempts at rebellion were bloody but brief.

"The Indians here, as more come, become humbler, and the gentiles [unconverted] show greater desire to be baptized."
—Father Luis Jayme, in a report to Serra

Old Town: It took many years for San Diego to reach this modest stature.

The attack ended at dawn, and the warriors scattered, taking with them statues of the Purissima Concepción and of San José, neither of which was ever seen again. Meanwhile, the garrison on Presidio Hill saw the haze of smoke from the fires below.

The presidio itself was not attacked. The warriors had crept up the hill, but fearful that the larger presidio guard might be already alerted, they hesitated to strike. By the time the soldiers rushed down the hill to the mission, it was all over. The grieving mission people gathered their wounded and dead, and returned to the presidio.

Within weeks, many Kumeyaay leaders were tracked down and brought in. Punishment was swift and brutal, and one warrior committed suicide rather than face a fatal flogging.

Rebuilding: Despite the attack, the missionaries were still determined to win the trust and faith of the Kumeyaay. So several months later they returned to the burnt-out ruins by the river and built a second mission of wood and thatch smeared with mud to foil the flaming arrows of the Indians. There was talk of war around the Kumeyaay campfires again in 1778. But the Spanish learned of the plot and reacted immediately by bringing the

A Short History of San Diego

plotters to the presidio in irons. In 1784, feeling secure, the priests built a third church, a fine building of solid adobe and timber.

But other problems threatened the mission. There were years when the normally placid San Diego River, swollen with rains and mountain snowmelt, became a deadly torrent. The crops in the riverbed seemed either to be washed away or seared by the sun. Then there were years of drought, when the river shrank to a muddy trickle. In 1803, an earthquake destroyed the church. The ground was cleared, the adobe was salvaged from the rubble, and a fourth church, the one we know today, was built.

The mission prospered slowly. Fields of wheat and barley were planted, and olive and date trees offered their shade. The San Diego River was tamed by a dam built six miles upstream in 1807. By the early 1830s, 15,000 head of cattle and 20,000 sheep grazed the hillsides. The bells in the mission tower called 1500 faithful Indians to prayer. In the church, an Indian choir sang Latin chants. Of all the long chain of missions marching up the length of California, San Diego enjoyed one of the largest congregations.

It has been argued by some historians that, while the missions were testimonies to Spanish perseverance, they also represented a terrible loss of heritage for the Indians. For centuries, the Indians had traveled the land according to the seasons. But at the missions they were settled in permanent buildings with thick adobe walls. Occasionally, mission Indians, called "neophytes" by the Spanish, would wander off into the hills to live again among the "wild" unconverted tribes. But the mission guard would soon hunt them down and return them to the strange, dictatorial world of regimented hours, work quotas, and bells calling the faithful to worship. At night, the mission Indians were locked in their rooms. Discipline was harsh; the whip and shackles were not unknown. And a way of life that had come from time unremembered vanished in a few generations.

The Indians were also ravaged by foreign diseases to which they had no immunity; converts died in great numbers from such simple European illnesses as the measles. The priests buried them in mass graves and listed the sad totals in ledgers. In 1800, mission records showed that of some 16,000 Indians who had been baptized in a ten-year period, approximately 9,000 had died.

Still, even though there were failures and sorrow, there were also times of joy. The ancient seasonal cycle of hunger and plenty was broken, as the priests taught their charges to plant, store, and grow fruit. The Indians learned new skills to make their way in Spanish California: husbandry, metal-working, stone-cutting. They shared a common Spanish language which allowed them to speak with tribes they could not understand before. For the first time, for example, the Indians of San Diego could talk with the Indians of San Juan

San Diego de Alcalá (1769) was the first of the 21 missions built along the Camino Real while San Francisco Solano (1823), north of San Francisco, was the last.

Capistrano. And always the priests offered what they felt to be the most precious gift of all, their faith.

C rumbling Walls: The dissolving of the missions began with Mexico's independence from Spain in 1821. The new government in Mexico City attempted to exploit its northern domains by issuing vast land grants. Thus the bureaucrats accomplished what warring Indians, flood, drought, disease, hunger, and earthquakes could not. They broke the power of the missions. The death blow came with the Secularization Act of 1833, when the church lands were broken up and put into private hands. Huge *ranchos* were carved from the mission holdings, creating cattle kingdoms that stretched for miles.

On September 20, 1834, San Diego's mission was put into the hands of government commissioner Juan José Rocha. In turning over the mission records, the last padre, Father Fernando Martín, ruefully pointed out that the military still owed the mission considerable money for supplies purchased or taken throughout the years. Mexican governor Pío Pico awarded the mission lands to a retired soldier and former *alcalde* (mayor) of San Diego named Santiago Arguello.

Foiled by the legal maneuvers of Californios, and then by the arrival of the Americans, Arguello was never really able to use the mission lands granted him.

In dissolving the mission system, the government announced that the Indians had been freed from the bondage of the missionaries. In reality, the Indians, irrevocably divorced from the land, scattered into the back country or wandered destitute in the streets of San Diego. In late 1833, Father Narciso Durán expressed his suspicions about why certain Californios enthusiastically agreed to the "freeing" of the Indians: "The government wants the Indians to be private owners of lands and other property; this is just. The Indians, however, want the freedom of vagabonds. The others [Californios] want the absolute liberation and emancipation of the neophytes without the command to form civilized towns, in order that they may avail themselves of the mission lands and other property . . . ."

Though the mission was officially transferred to government control in 1834, the priests carried on as best they could for more than a decade. In August, 1846, Father Vicente Oliva showed Marine Captain Archibald Gillespie a "large square of houses and a corral, a house for the padre and one for the servants and working people, several store houses and offices, and a large church with ancient and rich ornaments." Later that year Father Oliva moved to San Juan Capistrano, and the doors of the mission were closed at last.

Roof tiles from the mission buildings were pried off and taken away to cover roofs in what is now Old Town. The adobe walls of the mission buildings

A Short History of San Diego

Mother of the California Missions: Crumbling adobe walls in this late 19th century photograph hint at the size of Mission San Diego in its glory.

melted back into the earth. Meanwhile, the congregation saved what it could, moving the church vestments and art into the large Old Town home of Don José Antonio Estudillo. For several decades the mission bells hung forlornly from a wooden beam in Estudillo's garden. Other objects were hidden by devout Indians; Estudillo found silver candlesticks and chalices carefully buried in the earth near the ruins.

Shortly after the Mexican-American War, the United States military heaped one last indignity on the sad old buildings when they used the Mission San Diego as a cavalry barracks. In October, 1857, editor John Judson Ames of the *Herald* rode out to the mission. He found it "deserted and crumbling to decay . . . the place in the Church where once stood the Altar is now occupied by grim-visaged men of war. The cross, that sacred emblem consecrated to this temple of the Most High, has been taken down and cut up to light the evening campfires of the soldiers."

The Unbroken Chain: In 1862, 14 years after California had been taken by the United States as a prize of the Mexican-American War, President Abraham Lincoln restored the San Diego mission to the Catholic Church, including the 22 acres surrounding the buildings. Though Father Antonio Ubach established an Indian school there in 1900, the deterioration of the mission buildings continued. By the 1920s, little remained but a crumbling facade. In 1931, however, with funds provided by local citizens and a grant from the Hearst Foundation, the main mission buildings were restored. Five bells were hung in the bell tower; four were original while the fifth and largest was cast in 1894 from the cracked remnants of bells brought by the missionaries. Further restoration of the mission was delayed by the Depression and World War II.

In *The Franciscan Missions of California*, John Berger noted that, while the main church was completely restored, "little else remains of the buildings, though adobe ruins suggest their extent and location. Only one adobe room still stands, sadly neglected and desolate. The front wall of the monastery has been replaced by an unsightly wooden fence. Before that wall in mission days ran the pillared cloister. But today the 'Mother of the Missions' pitifully reflects a remiss negligence which civic pride should recognize."

Largely restored today, Mission San Diego de Alcalá is the center of a busy and active parish, visited each year by thousands of tourists and San Diegans. Modern Mission Valley is filled with businesses and stores, and posh condominiums rise across the street from the mission doors. The haze from the cooking fires of the Kumeyaay has been replaced by the smoke of backyard barbecues.

Yet Father Jayme, who now rests beneath the stones of the mission sanctuary, must surely be at peace. The ringing of mission bells rises clear above the din of the Mission Valley shopping centers, hotels, restaurants, and the roar of traffic from nearby Highway 8. Each day the Angelus is rung, signaling a time for personal reflection and prayer. There is still the call to Mass on Sunday. The faithful come; the chain is unbroken.

In 1976, Pope Paul VI honored the mission with the title of minor basilica.

But today's visitors often forget that the mission was more than an outpost of faith. It was also an outpost of empire, part of a carefully thought-out plan to colonize and hold California for the Spanish crown. Even as the priests were struggling to build their mission on the banks of the San Diego River, secular men were at work strengthening the colony's defenses.

The Golden Hills

5

In the early 1800s, California consisted of a few struggling settlements perched on the edge of a vast wilderness. At Monterey, Santa Barbara, and San Diego, presidios and missions stood near the coast. The Mission San Gabriel rose a few miles inland from what is now Los Angeles. Almost 200 miles north, hidden behind the coastal ranges of the central coast, Mission San Antonio was built amid clusters of oak trees. It was at the founding of Mission San Antonio in July, 1771, that an exuberant Father Serra rang a bell hung from a tree, crying, "Oh ye gentiles! Come, come to the holy Church!"When others in the party pointed out that the church had yet to be built, Serra answered, "Let me give vent to my heart which desires that this bell be heard all over the world."

But while Serra considered California a garden of souls waiting to be harvested, others had more earthly concerns. Isolated from the Spanish empire, California had to offer safe ports for the Manila galleons and produce its own food and goods in order to prove its worth. The first step in ending California's isolation was to establish a more direct land route from Mexico's mainland supply bases. Until that route was established, all supplies and communications had to come by sea or be carried up the length of Baja California.

In December, 1773, a column of 32 soldiers and muleskinners set out to cross the bleached bone deserts of Arizona into California. At the head of the column was Captain Juan Bautista de Anza, a third-generation frontier soldier known for his exploits against the Apaches.

Anza arrived at the Mission San Gabriel near Los Angeles in early 1774. "We found here four friars, its missionaries, from the College of San Fernando de Mexico, who welcomed us with unrestrained jubilation and demonstrations

Opposite page
Vaqueros: **Californios were famed for their bravado and horsemanship.**

of joy, with solemn peal of bells and the chanting of the Te Deum . . . This was all the more pleasing to them because it was so unexpected, for they had not had any news, except very remote, of this expedition, which they had considered impracticable even for a hundred men."

Eight years later, Don Juan Pantoja, chief pilot on the frigate *La Princesa*, produced the first detailed charts of San Diego Bay, ensuring safe anchorages for Spain's ships. It was on Pantoja's maps that the headland at the bay's mouth was first called "Point Loma," by which name it is still known today. Another part of the shore noted by Pantoja and still seen on modern maps is a reminder of the high cost of exploration. Several of Pantoja's fellow sailors died while in San Diego, and were buried at the muddy foot of today's Market Street. Most of those who walk today along that part of the waterfront with its colorful restaurants and shops are unaware of its sad name: Dead Man's Point.

Some claim that Dead Man's Point was named in 1769 for the dead sailors of the *San Carlos* and *San Antonio*. But those ships anchored farther up the bay, and most historians conclude that the point was named for Pantoja's dead.

Vancouver Calls: As the non-Spanish world became aware of California, plans were prepared for the defense of its harbors. That those defenses might one day be needed became apparent in November, 1793, when the Spanish were stunned by the arrival in San Diego Bay of three British warships under the command of Captain George Vancouver. The Spanish offered the English a polite if cautious welcome. Visits were exchanged and appropriate toasts made.

Meanwhile, Vancouver made careful notes on San Diego's defenses:

> The Presidio of San Diego [is] garrisoned by a company of 60 men . . . These soldiers are all very expert horsemen, and, so far as their numbers extend, are well qualified to support themselves against any domestic insurrection; but are totally incapable of making any resistance against a foreign invasion. With little difficulty San Diego might also be rendered a place of considerable strength, by establishing a small force at the entrance to the port; where, at this time, there were neither works, guns, houses or other habitations nearer than the presidio, which is at the distance of at least five miles from the port, and where they have only three small pieces of brass cannon.

Before leaving, Vancouver presented the priests with a small pump organ. The missionaries generously responded. At Santa Barbara alone, 20 pack mule loads of fresh fruits and vegetables were delivered to the English ships.

The English were mystified by Spain's weak effort to expand its hold on California. "Why such an extent of territory should have been thus subjugated, and after all the expense and labor that has been bestowed upon its colonization turned to no account whatever, is a mystery in the science of the state policy not easily to be explained."

Almost as if in answer to the English observations on San Diego's defense, Pablo Sanchez of the Spanish Royal Corps of Engineers reported in July, 1795,

"Nothing has been done at the Port of San Diego, where ... a battery of 8 twelve-pounders should be located on the point called Guijarros, opposite the entrance. But since the peninsula is barren, various difficulties may be presented in the construction of the battery; in San Diego there is a lack of construction materials, particularly wood. The battery here is going to cost more than it would if the circumstances were more favorable."

Soon after, materials and workmen arrived from Monterey to add buildings to the Presidio and construct a small fortress on Guijarros, today called Ballast Point. In addition, San Diego's garrison was enlarged to 90 men. By 1800, San Diego, though far from impregnable, was no longer as defenseless as the English had found it.

In 1803, Fort Guijarros' new guns fired on the *Lelia Byrd;* the first of a growing number of smuggling ships that bedeviled the Spanish. Its captains, Cleveland and Shaler, were the first Americans to see San Diego

The Russians: In 1806, Nikolai Rezanov, a Russian diplomat who had spent two months at San Francisco, prepared a report for the Russian-American Company. Like Vancouver, Rezanov saw imperialist opportunity in Spain's feebleness:

If the [Czarist] government had given earlier thought to this part of the world . . . then one could positively maintain that New California would never have become a Spanish possession . . . Today there is only an unoccupied stretch [north of San Francisco], so useful to us and quite necessary, and if we should allow it to slip out of our grasp, what will posterity say? We shall be able little by little to expand farther south to the port of San Francisco which marks the boundary of California . . . If only the means are provided for the early beginnings of this plan, I can boldly say that we . . . shall have so consolidated our position at the end of ten years as ever to have in mind the coast of California and, at the slightest concurrence of favorable political circumstances in Europe, include it among the Russian possession.

Rezanov died in 1807. But his urgings bore fruit, and in 1812 the Russians built Fort Ross on the fogbound coast north of San Francisco. Ten cannon were mounted on the fort's redwood walls and the double-headed eagle of Imperial Russia flew assertively from the flagpole. The Spanish government twice ordered the Russians to leave and were twice refused. Spain had acted too late in trying to build up its California colony. Her garrisons were weak and widely separated, and the missions, while beginning to prosper, were not enough to hold the land. In Mexico, revolution against Spanish rule was simmering. The Spanish could not force the Russians to leave and, in fact, it was only a matter of time before the rest of California slipped from Spain's grasp.

Rezanov's romance with the Presidio *commandante*'s 15-year-old daughter, his premature death, and her grieved entry into a convent have become California legend. The Russian count's official report shows, though, that his ardor was purely cynical.

Independence: The Mexican War of Independence came to a close in September, 1821. With it, Spanish rule ended in California. Isolated, far from the center of conflict, California received the news with disbelief. In Monterey, Governor Vicente de Solá wrote, "Independence is a dream." After all, he went on, the empire was "immortal, incomparable." On San Diego's Presidio Hill, the scarlet and gold flag of Imperial Spain continued to fly.

Finally, sometime between September, 1823, and January, 1824, the Spanish flag was lowered; the Mexican flag with its Aztec eagle and snake was raised in its place. The next day, the few dozen soldiers of the garrison cut off their short queues tied with scarlet ribbon, the sign of a king's soldier. In the months following independence, increasing numbers of settlers came down the hill from the presidio and built homes in what is now called "Old Town." A village came into being, complete with a dusty plaza, school of 18 students, and small gardens.

Eager to keep Alta California, the new government in Mexico City dispatched a stream of grand schemes and pronouncements. For a while there was talk of reviving the fabled Manila galleons. But colonization was the surest and cheapest way to Mexicanize the region. One observer, Scots merchant Alexander Forbes, was not impressed with the new settlers. In an 1839 book on California, he grumbled, "They were of every class of persons except that which could be useful . . . there was not one agriculturist amongst them. They

The earliest of Old Town's historical buildings, built in 1820 by a Captain Ruiz, is now the clubhouse of the Presidio Park Golf Course. Two Mexican-era adobes, the 1827 Estudillo and 1835 Machado-Stewart, have been restored as part of the Old Town San Diego State Historic Park.

Fierce Pride: In a photograph taken a quarter of a century after the American conquest, Jose Serrano's face still reflects the pride of the Californio rancher. Serrano fought the Americans at San Pasqual in 1846.

A Short History of San Diego

Pilgrim: Richard Henry Dana opened American eyes to the Far West.

were chiefly from the city of Mexico, and consisted of artisans and idlers who had been made to believe that they would soon enrich themselves in idleness in this happy country."

San Diegan Juan Bandini disagreed. "The persons who came to California as colonists belonged in general to the artisan class so that there were carpenters, farm workers, silver smiths, tailors, shoe makers, hat makers, and others who, in spite of what is said, were to be and have been of service to the country."

Yankee Traders: Trading by New England seafarers had been a furtive affair under the Spanish. But under the more relaxed Mexicans it became big business. There was money to be made in cowhides and tallow for Yankee trader and Californio rancher alike. In the late 1820s, a single cowhide was worth one American dollar. By the 1830s, the price had risen to two dollars, and by the early 1840s, a cowhide was worth four. Each cow also provided an average of 200 pounds of tallow. In the five years from 1831 to 1836, the Boston firm of Bryant and Sturgis imported about 500,000 California cowhides.

Around 1830, some of the *Brookline's* sailors stitched together an American flag from scraps. When they raised it over their storehouse, the Mexican authorities were not amused and ordered it taken down.

In 1829, men from the ship *Brookline* out of Boston built a storehouse for the hides they purchased in San Diego. Others soon followed suit. American trade goods flowed into California, and life for the wealthy Californio ranchers took on a new elegance. Fine china appeared on rancho tables, and cow hides returned as high fashion shoes.

To some New Englanders, the Californio hunger for luxury goods was foolish, though profitable. In March, 1835, the trading ship *Pilgrim* put into San Diego with a cargo of what crewman Richard Henry Dana called, "Everything that can be imagined, from Chinese fireworks to English cartwheels." Dana, who was 19 at the time, was not impressed with the Californios. In his celebrated 1840 book *Two Years Before the Mast*, he wrote:

> The Californians are an idle, thriftless people and can make nothing for themselves. The country abounds in grapes, yet they buy bad wines made in Boston and brought round by us, at an immense price, and retail it among themselves at a *real* [a *real* was around 12½ cents] by the small wine glass. Their hides, too, which they value at two dollars in money, they give for something which costs 75 cents in Boston; and buy shoes (like as not, made of their own hides, and which have been carried twice around Cape Horn) at three or four dollars, and 'chicken skin' boots at 15 dollars apiece. Things sell, on an average, at an advance of nearly 300 percent upon the Boston prices.

Californio Juan Bandini admitted, "The great weakness of the Californians, as far as the economy is concerned, is that they spend more on dress than they should . . . I think that no country in the world will spend as much on clothes as the Californians do."

As more Americans came to California to trade and settle, the Mexican government grew concerned that the trickle of *Yanquis* might swell into a stream. On New Year's Day in 1827, a stranger rode into San Diego and suddenly there was more reason for concern.

Mountain Man: Jedediah Smith's 1827 visit alarmed San Diego's authorities.

Mountain Men: The stranger was Jedediah Smith, one of the most fabled of the West's mountain men. To the astonishment of the Californios, Smith announced that he and his party of trappers had crossed the blazing Mojave desert to San Gabriel near Los Angeles and had then ridden south to San Diego. Horrified that the mountains and deserts guarding California's eastern flanks had been conquered, the Mexican authorities banished Smith from the province. But others soon followed his trail.

One of those was Kentuckian Sylvester Pattie, who marched from Santa Fe in 1828 with a party of eight trappers including his son, James Ohio. The mood of the authorities had grown darker since Smith's visit. The trappers were jailed in San Diego on charges of espionage. They were released a few months later, though the elder Pattie had died in prison.

That same year another American ship, the *Franklin*, fought her way out of the harbor past Fort Guijarros as had the *Lelia Byrd* a quarter of a century before. The fort was undamaged but the *Franklin* left with two ugly holes in her hull and part of her rigging shot away.

Californios: Mexico tried to promote the colonization of its northern reaches by granting liberal land grants to settlers. The romantic era of the vast land-grant ranchos lasted less than three decades, and ended with the American conquest in 1847. Land was plentiful and boundaries were approximate, sometimes noted as *mas o menos* (more or less). The first San Diego rancho, 8,400-acre Rancho Los Penasquitos, was granted in 1823 to Captain Francisco Ruíz, former commander of the San Diego garrison. Some of the ranchos were quite small; La Cañada de Los Coches, awarded in 1843 to Doña Apolinaria Lorenzana, was less than 30 acres. Others, like the sprawling 133,440-acre Rancho Santa Margarita y Las Flores a few miles north of what is now Oceanside, became great cattle kingdoms.

Twice a year the *vaqueros* gathered to ride across their golden hills. In springtime, calves were rounded up for branding; in the fall came the *matanza*, the slaughter. There was also time for *fiestas* and *fandangos* that might last a week or more. The Californios danced, and held cockfights and riding exhibitions. Food and drink were plentiful. An old Californio lady recalled years later to Benjamin Hayes, "It was the reign of prosperity and plenty."

In 1833 Mexico enacted the Secularization Act, which broke up the mission land holdings. With this boon, many of the ranchos grew even larger. The Indians who had lived on the mission lands suddenly found themselves lost in a world that had little use for them.

In May, 1833, Father Narciso Durán was in Los Angeles, where he saw some of the Indians who had been pushed from the missions. He observed sadly:

> Beyond comparison, they live far more wretched and oppressed than those [still] in the missions. There is not one who has a garden of his own, or a yoke of oxen, a horse, or a house fit for a rational being . . . I saw with mine own eyes . . . the poor Indians sweeping the street . . . and I was told they do the same for their livelihood. For offenses which the white people consider small, or as nothing among themselves, those Indians are placed over a cannon and given one hundred blows on the naked body . . . All in reality are slaves, or servants of white men.

Some major California land holdings, notably the Irvine Ranch (a combination of three ranchos), date from the days of the land grants.

"The Californios all appear to be gentlemen of the first class . . . I make a very grotesque appearance when seated at the table amidst the dandys with their ruffles, silks and broad cloths."
—Harrison Rogers, mountain man, December, 1826

In the late 1830s, some Indians, their bravery fed by desperation, began to raid outlying ranchos. Livestock disappeared and travelers into the interior were no longer safe. There were nights when *vaqueros* looked nervously at horizons lit by faint pink as distant ranch houses went up in flames.

By 1837, the Indians were boldly raiding near San Diego. A creamery was attacked and looted in the El Cajon Valley, and three Christian Indian workmen were murdered. In April, Rancho Jamul was attacked. Four men were killed and two young girls were kidnapped and never seen again.

A **Small Village:** On January 1, 1835, San Diego became a civil pueblo. The Mexican population had grown to over 400 with ranching and trade as the main occupations. Juan Osuna was elected the first *alcalde*, a combination mayor and justice of the peace.

As *alcalde*, Osuna enjoyed considerable power. Another *alcalde*, Walter Colton of Monterey, later wrote, "This office . . . involves every breach of the peace, every case of crime, every business obligation, and every disputed land title within a space of 300 miles . . . such an absolute disposal of questions affecting property and personal liberty never ought to be confided to one man. There is not a judge on any bench in England or the United States whose power is so absolute as that of the *alcalde*."

Despite Mexico's efforts to secure it, the United States was becoming increasingly interested in California. U.S. Navy warships prowled the sea off the California coast, and, in 1842 Commodore Thomas ap Catesby Jones seized Monterey. The city was released only after Jones learned to his embarrassment that war with Mexico had not yet been declared.

An 1844 book by Robert Greenhow, *The History of Oregon and California*, described San Diego as enjoying, "Trade . . . probably greater than that of any other place in California. [It] is a small village, situated about a mile north of the bay. The presidio is a mud fort, two miles further inland; besides which, there are some fortifications capable of commanding the entrance of the port. The mission is a distant seven miles from the presidio, in a valley, through which a torrent of fine water rushes during the rainy season."

On the title page of Greenhow's book was an ominous statement for the Californios: "The possible destiny of the United States of America, as a nation of a hundred million of freemen, stretching from the Atlantic to the Pacific, living under the laws of Alfred, and speaking the language of Shakespeare and Milton, is an august conception."

By 1845 congressmen were riding on a wave of "Manifest Destiny," thundering that the United States was ordained to cover the continent from sea to sea. The American consul in Monterey, Thomas O. Larkin, received secret orders to encourage California's annexation to the United States. In 1846, the American army crossed the Mexican border and started its march to Mexico City. The Mexican-American War had begun.

Unlike the portion of that war fought in Mexico, there would be no massed ranks or grand strategies in the taking of California. Instead there would be a series of quick, vicious fights in places like Sonoma, Los Angeles, and San Gabriel. The biggest battle in California would be fought on a cold, rainy morning in a valley a few miles east of San Diego called San Pasqual.

The fabled Bear Flag Republic, formed in Sonoma in June, 1846, was irrelevant to San Diego—as it was for California as a whole, despite legend.

Death On a Rainy Morning

6

In the beginning, the conquest of California came easily. Lost in the backwater of the Mexican-American War, California seemed for a time destined to fall to the American invaders without a battle. On the warm summer morning of July 7, 1846, Marines landed at Monterey. Within an hour, they had raised the American flag. The bay echoed to the rumble of a 21-gun salute from American warships. A proclamation from Commodore John Sloat, commander of the U.S. naval forces in the Pacific, was read from in front of the customs house: "I declare to the inhabitants of California that, although I come in arms with a powerful force, I do not come among them as an enemy of California; on the contrary, I come as their best friend, as hence forward California will be a portion of the United States, and its peaceful inhabitants will enjoy the same rights and privileges as citizens of any other portion of that territory."

The U.S. forces took California quickly while the Californios either stood by or vanished into the hills. By the end of July, 1846, Yerba Buena (soon to be renamed San Francisco), Sacramento, Bodega, and Sonoma were under American control. On August 13, the American flag was raised over Los Angeles without opposition. A garrison of 50 men under Marine Captain Archibald Gillespie took up its post as the bulk of the American forces moved elsewhere.

The first weeks of the California conquest came without battle, but not without bloodshed. Lieutenant Archibald MacRae wrote an angry letter home to his brother:

Two troops of mounted men, the command of which was given to two Pursers for God knows what reason, not being able to amuse themselves in any other way, have been cooly shooting down some peaceful and friendly Indians. This occurred just before we left and therefore I do not know the full particulars, but all accounts

Opposite page
Clash of Arms: A contemporary American watercolor captures the fury of the Battle of San Pasqual.

agree upon the fact that deliberate murders have been committed upon a number of men who, under the impression that they were to be put to death when ordered to arrange themselves in a line in front of the troop, committed the very grave offense of attempting to escape, and who committed no other fault.

Later in his letter, Lieutenant MacRae analyzed why California had been taken with what seemed such little effort: "The country is very thinly populated and the few Californians in it are divided . . . into three or four factions, so that any number of resolute men . . . can do what they please . . . As for the towns on the coast, all put together would not be a match for one good frigate."

U **nder Mexico Alone:** Meanwhile, in Los Angeles, Captain Gillespie was busily giving the Californios a bitter taste of military occupation. The city was put under martial law, enforced by Marine patrols. A strict curfew was established. No two Californios were to be found walking together in the streets. All amusements and parties were banned.

"Gillespie was so obstinate toward these people that he became a hateful tyrant."
—Coronel, a "thoroughly trustworthy" Californio

The citizens of Los Angeles soon revolted. In late September, 1846, Gillespie and his marines found themselves besieged by angry Californios under Captain José María Flores. A proclamation signed by 300 Californios was issued:

> We, all the inhabitants of the Department of California, as members of the great Mexican nation, our desire has been and is to stand, free and independent, under Mexico alone. The authorities established by the invader are illegitimate. We swear not to lay down our arms until the enemy has been expelled from our soil. Every Mexican citizen from 15 years of age to 60 who does not take up arms to carry out the plan will be declared a traitor under pain of death. Any Mexican or foreigner who directly or indirectly aids the enemy will suffer the same penalty. All property of every American resident who has directly or indirectly aided the enemy will be confiscated. Those who oppose this plan will be shot.

The American force surrendered on September 20 and was allowed to march to San Pedro where Gillespie had promised they would board ships and leave. However, Gillespie was met at San Pedro by the American warship *Vandalia* and 350 marines and sailors. Thus reinforced, he turned about, determined to retake Los Angeles. But at the "Battle of the Old Woman's Gun" on the Dominguez Rancho just outside the pueblo, the Americans were thrown back with five dead and several wounded.

The "old woman's gun" was dug up from her garden and used to good effect by the Californios.

California flared into revolt. At the Battle of Natividad in the Salinas Valley in November, the Americans were again bloodied with four dead. The small American garrison at Santa Barbara abandoned the town and marched north to

A Short History of San Diego

Monterey. At San Diego, the American garrison fled to the safety of a whaling ship, leaving the Californios to reoccupy the land from Santa Barbara to San Diego.

Manifest Destiny:
Commodore John Sloat
raised the American flag over
Monterey on July 7, 1846.

In late 1846, however, the Americans received good news. The U.S. First Dragoons, called the "Army of the West" and led by a hardened frontier officer named Stephen Watts Kearny, had arrived. By December 5, they were camped within a day's ride of San Diego. Near their camp was a broad, flat valley called San Pasqual.

The March Westward: General Kearny's Army of the West had set out six months before from Fort Leavenworth, Kansas, with 1500 men and 16 cannon. After weeks of swirling dust and 110 degree temperatures, they raised the U.S. flag in the plaza at Santa Fe and New Mexico became an American possession.

At Santa Fe, Kearny split his forces as instructed by the War Department: "When you arrive at Santa Fe . . . you may find yourself in a condition to garrison it with part of your command . . . with the remainder, press forward to California."

Actually, Kearny split his forces at Santa Fe into thirds. He sent the First Missouri Mounted Volunteers south to Chihuahua, Mexico, where they joined General John Wool's division in a battle against the northern Mexican armies. He left a garrison in Santa Fe and, with 300 troopers, rode west to take California.

On the upper Rio Grande, Kearny came across the celebrated mountain man Kit Carson riding eastward with important dispatches. It was all over, Carson said. California had already been taken, not that there had been much of a fight. It appeared, Carson grumbled, that the Californios weren't much for fighting. "They would never expose themselves to an attack," he complained, "for they have a holy terror of the American rifle!"

There was disappointment in Kearny's ranks at having missed the war. "Most of us hoped," wrote staff surgeon Dr. John Griffin, "that we would have a little kick up with the good people of California but this totally blasted all our hopes."

Kearny again split his forces, sending the dispatches on to Washington. Two hundred of his men left for the war still raging in the south. Taking Carson as guide, he set out for California with 100 tired men and two battered cannon. Two months later his small command would be fighting for its life at San Pasqual.

The battle of San Pasqual happened by chance. The Californios were searching for American foraging parties from San Diego when Kearny's force offered a much more tempting target.

Near San Diego they were joined by 40 sailors and marines who had ridden up from the harbor. Kearny and his men were told they were needed after all, for California was in revolt. In fact, Kearny was warned, there were armed Californios waiting in the valley just ahead.

The campaign, stretched into six months, had sapped much of the troopers' enthusiasm. Many of their horses were dead; instead they rode mules. Their weapons were rusted and worn, their uniforms tattered. It had rained during the night and much of their gunpowder was soaked and useless. The Army of the West was only a ghost of the powerful force that had set out from Fort Leavenworth.

Voices Shouting: In the predawn darkness of December 6, 1846, Kearny sent out scouts to probe the Californios' position. but as the scouts neared the Californio camp, a dog barked and a voice called, "*Quien vive?*" With the Californios alerted, the scouts fell back. There could be no surprise attack now. Kearny grimly prepared to charge. The rain had faded into a cold mist. Forming a column of twos in the dawn, the Americans started down the valley. Andrés Pico and over 100 Californios waited across the valley. Mounted on their well-bred horses, they carried few guns. Instead, they carried lariats that could lash out like a rattlesnake and pull a man from his horse. In their hands they held eight-foot-long willow lances tipped with metal points.

An Indian girl named Felicita watched from a hill overlooking the valley. Many decades later she remembered seeing the battle begin:

> We heard the sounds of voices shouting on the mountainside toward Santa Maria; we ran out of our huts to find the cause. The clouds hung so low that at first we could see nothing for the mist, but soon there were the figures of men, like shadows, riding down the mountain. As they drew nearer, we could see that they were soldiers, wearing coats of blue.
>
> The Mexican [Californio] soldiers were sitting on their horses, holding their long lances in their hands; they now rode swiftly to meet the soldiers in blue, and soon there came the sounds of battle. But the Indians, in great fear, fled again to the mountains. When we had climbed high above the valley, we hid behind the brush and weeds. Then we looked down and watched.

Even as an old woman, Felicita remembred the fear:

> There were days when the Mexican soldiers rode through San Pasqual on their beautiful horses. They came from the presidio at San Diego and carried swords and lances. At the sight of them, women and children ran to hide in the brush and rocks of the hills, for these men counted our lives of little worth and we feared them.
>
> One of our men who had lived at the mission told us that these strange soldiers from the hills were Americans and that they were fighting to take the land away from the Mexicans. The Mexicans had not been good to the Indians, so we were not sorry to see the new soldiers come against them.

Stephen Kearny: His instructions read, "Press forward to California."

Captain Johnson's Charge: Captain Johnson and 12 dragoons reached the valley floor first. Kearny ordered them to a trot. But in the confusion the order was misunderstood, and Johnson signaled a charge. The tired horses broke into a run. Horrified, Kearny watched the 13 troopers ride away from the main force to a barrage of Californio gunfire from across the valley. Leandro Osuna fired—Johnson rolled from his saddle with a bullet in his forehead. Nearby, a dragoon also fell dead into the mud.

Moments later, the rest of the American column slammed into the Californios. Battle was joined. Kit Carson's horse went down, throwing the scout into a bone-jarring heap and breaking his rifle. The Americans tried to fire their guns and found them useless because of wet powder. They slashed

The Battle of San Pasqual was one of the few times when soldiers in the west were forced to use the saber. Throughout the Indian wars that followed, the Indians, like the Californios, used expert horsemanship to avoid the blade's vicious sweep.

Lancer: Despite his rather dandified appearance in this watercolor, the Californio lancer was a formidable fighter.

out desperately with their sabers, but blades were as useless as wet gunpowder against the long Californio lances.

These were used with terrible effect, dancing in and out of the American ranks, stabbing at the dragoons and pushing them from their horses. Lariats whistled through the air, pulling Americans off their horses and dragging them to the ground where Californios pierced them.

Suddenly, incredibly, the Californios broke off their attack. The Americans could not believe it. The Californios were actually retreating!

With Johnson dead, Captain B.D. Moore took command of the point. Not wanting to give the Californios a chance to regroup, he ordered a second charge. The dragoons advanced in a long ragged line across the valley.

From behind a small hill, the Californios sprang their trap, lances levelled. There had been no retreat; they had just withdrawn to reform their ranks. The American charge was abruptly shattered into small fragments. John Stanley, a draftsman on Kearny's staff, remembered, "The Californians . . . fought with desperation, making great havoc with their lances, crying, *'Viva Mexico! Viva California!'* It was a real hand-to-hand fight, and lasted half an hour."

Moore, in the lead, got one pistol shot off and then went down with two lance wounds. Moments later, a Californio bullet put him out of his misery. Near him young Lieutenant Thomas Hammond sprawled dead in the mud.

A Short History of San Diego

Cut off from his men, Kearny fought on alone. A veteran of the War of 1812 with almost 30 years on the frontier, Kearny was a tough and capable soldier; he was weakened from three wounds. The Californios closed in on him. But Lieutenant William Emory of the Topographical Engineers was at his side, and they beat off the attackers.

The Californios were renowned for their ability with the lariat. A favorite sport was to rope wild bears and drag them home to fight bulls in the ring.

Gillespie Joins the Fight: Just then, Captain Archibald Gillespie appeared on the edge of the battlefield. He had ridden up from San Diego to meet Kearny with 40 marines and sailors. He plunged into the swirling battle crying, "Rally, men, for God's sake, rally, follow me!"

The Californios turned on him with delight. They knew and loathed Gillespie from his brief but harsh occupation of Los Angeles. He swiftly parried off the first lances but was thrown to the ground. Stumbling to his feet, he took a lance full in the chest. Again he tried to rise but was slammed back by a lance thrust at his face, cutting his lip badly and breaking a tooth. He lay in the mud as a Californio horse leaped over him. Then the lancers turned away and he was alone. Gillespie slowly made his way to safety.

On the edge of the battle, desperate American gunners tried to bring their artillery into action. Californios thundered up to the cannon. One gunner took refuge behind his gun carriage but the lancers found him. A lariat sailed through the air, encircling a howitzer. The Americans watched helplessly as their gun was dragged away through the rocks and scrub.

One of the American guns, called the "Sutter Gun," had been part of the Russian defenses at Fort Ross.

Though weak from loss of blood, Archibald Gillespie was still determined to be in the thick of battle. He held a cigar lighter to one of the last cannons. The gun fired, and Gillespie sank unconscious into the mud.

As if signaled by the blast, the Californios scattered across the valley and out of range. The Americans found themselves alone on the battlefield with their dead and dying. The entire action had taken less than 20 minutes. In that time a fifth of Kearny's command had been wiped out.

A Melancholy Picture: With the Californios gone, gunfire and screaming horses were replaced by the moans of wounded men. Eighteen lay dead, four others were dying. The nine other wounded, including the seemingly indestructible Gillespie, kept Army Doctor John Griffin hard at work. "When the General saw me, he told me that he was wounded and wished my services . . . I then met Captain Gillespie who told me he was wounded, he was bleeding profusely, the wound being directly over the heart. Captain Gibson next called me and in a few moments I had my hands full.

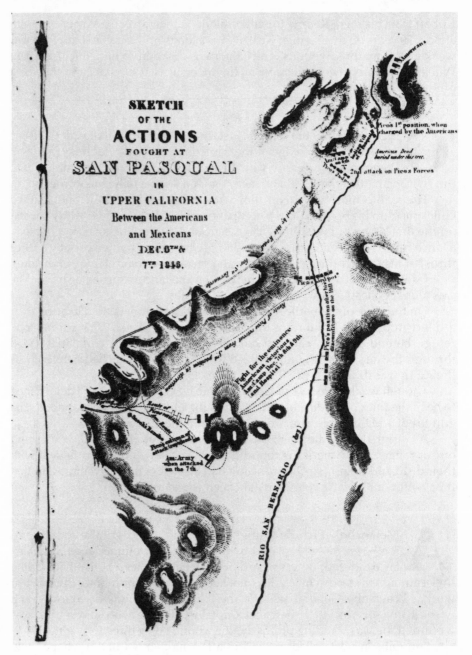

SKETCH
OF THE
ACTIONS
FOUGHT AT
SAN PASQUAL
IN
UPPER CALIFORNIA
Between the Americans
and Mexicans
DEC.6TH &
7TH 1846.

Battle: After the battle, American officers mapped the San Pasqual battlefield trying to figure out what went wrong.

When General Kearny realized the situation, he said, 'Go and dress the wounds of the soldiers who require more attention than I do and when you have done that, come to me.'" A few moments later, Kearny, weak from loss of blood, fainted.

In a letter written a little over a month later, draftsman John Stanley recalled, "We camped on the field and collected the dead. At first General Kearny thought to move on the same day. The dead were lashed on mules, and remained two hours or more in that posture. It was a sad and melancholy picture. We soon found, however, that our wounded were unable to travel. The mules were relieved of their packs, and the men engaged in fortifying the place for the night. During the day the enemy was in sight, curvetting their horses [making their horses prance], keeping our camp in constant excitement."

That night, December 6, 1846, the dead were buried in a mass grave beneath a willow. While the surviving Americans nursed their wounded, three couriers slipped away and rode to San Diego for help.

The next morning the battered column started for San Diego. But that afternoon Pico's lancers reappeared, fresh, rested, and ready to do battle. John Stanley remembered, "We had travelled about seven miles, when, just before sunset, we were attacked. The enemy came charging down a valley, about one hundred well-mounted men. They were about dividing their force, probably with a view of attacking us in the front and rear, when General Kearny ordered us to take possession of a hill on our left. The enemy, seeing the movement, struck for the same point, reaching it before us."

A number of dragoons under Lieutenant Emory charged the hill and drove the lancers off. Two Americans were wounded in the short fight. The Californios fell back, and the Americans took possession of their brief and vulnerable refuge.

Mule Hill: Exhausted, hungry, thirsty, with many of its wounded in agony, the Army of the West could go no further. The soldiers dug in. Rocks were gathered for barricades, and holes were gouged into the dry riverbed below the hill in search of water. Some of the faithful mules were killed to be roasted over bonfires and eaten. The place was given the melancholy name by which it is still known today: Mule Hill.

That night the Americans saw they were surrounded by campfires. Andrés Pico and his lancers now held the dragoons in a tight grip. The trapped soldiers could only hope that the couriers sent the night before had made it through enemy lines to San Diego.

With morning, a Californio approached under a flag of truce. The three couriers to San Diego had gotten through but on returning had been picked up by the Californios. Now Pico was proposing a prisoner exchange on a one-for-one basis.

However, the Americans held only one prisoner. Pablo Vejar happily rejoined his comrades. Half way down, he passed courier Thomas Burgess trudging up to what was left of the Army of the West.

Burgess brought discouraging news. Help would be sent, but it would take time. It seemed there was a shortage of horses in San Diego. When Gillespie and his volunteers had made their dash from the town to join Kearny, they had taken most of the available animals with them.

The situation on Mule Hill grew desperate. Kearny asked for three volunteers to carry another, more urgent plea to San Diego. Navy Lieutenant Edward Beale, frontiersman Kit Carson, and an unidentified Indian who had come from San Diego with Beale left that night.

The identity of the volunteer Indian remains a mystery. Some historians believe he may have been one of the Delaware Indians known to have been with Kearny, others that he may have come up from San Diego with Gillespie. He might also have been one of the many local Indians who hated and feared the Californios.

They came within a razor's edge of not making it. Recalled Carson, "We had to crawl about two miles. We could see three rows of sentinels, all ahorseback, we would often have to pass within 20 yards of one." Twelve miles from San Diego, they separated. The Indian arrived first, then Carson. Beale arrived last, in such wretched condition that he had to be carried.

The American Navy band was playing in the plaza that evening. In the Bandini House, a ball was being held, and music and laughter could be clearly heard. But with Beale's shocking arrival, the peaceful evening was shattered. Orders were snapped out, and officers took their posts. A relief column prepared to march at once.

Kearny was growing more certain that his latest pleas had not gotten through to San Diego. He grimly ordered the baggage destroyed to keep it from falling into Californio hands. The Americans prepared to fight their way out. A last meal of mule meat was prepared, thanks to the Californios who had earlier tried to stampede the Americans' stock by driving horses and mules through the camp. Dr. Griffin cheerfully wrote that one Mexican mule in particular was a "godsend to us for the mule was fat and that which we had been eating was not equal by any means to stall-fed beef, so we had mule soup for breakfast."

In all, 22 Americans and 11 Mexicans died in the action at San Pasqual.

Help: On the night of December 10, Kearny and his men heard the unreal sound of American voices in the distance. It was the relief column, 215 soldiers and marines on a forced march from San Diego. The siege was lifted. By morning, as the Americans prepared to move out, the Californio lancers had faded into the hills and into history.

On December 12, 1846, in a driving rain, the Army of the West at last entered San Diego. In the harbor was the reassuring sight of American warships at anchor: the *Portsmouth, Savannah,* and nearby, the powerful *Congress.* On the hill overlooking what is now Old Town, American artillery glowered from behind the earthworks of "Fort Stockton." San Diego was, and would remain, American.

The end for Mexican California came swiftly. On January 17, 1847, a way of life passed as Andrés Pico surrendered to Colonel John Charles Frémont.

The Californios rode in small bands down from the hills to surrender. Several of those who had fought at San Pasqual came to San Diego under a flag of truce. One of them was Leandro Osuna, who had killed Captain Johnson during the first charge. Osuna defiantly carried his lance, its tattered pennant stained with blood. The Americans took no revenge. The war was over.

Conquerers: Kit Carson (standing) was a hero at San Pasqual, and the peripatetic John Frémont took the Californio's surrender at Cahuenga in January, 1847.

The Mormons: The American military presence in San Diego grew steadily. The U.S.S. *Cyane,* whose marines had first raised the American flag over San Diego's plaza seven months before, returned with the New Year of 1847. Then, in March, Company B of the Mormon Battalion marched into San Diego. Arriving too late to take part in the war, the soldiers set to work building up the little settlement, digging wells and raising buildings. The local citizens were at first uneasy with the Mormons, a fact of which the men of Company B were aware. Many Californios expected a cruel military occupation. But, as the Mormon Battalion marching song said, they served "with willing heart and hand." When the Mormon enlistments ended a few months later, many San Diegans were genuinely sorry to see them leave and asked them to stay.

The Mormon Battalion was drafted into the Army at Council Bluffs, Iowa, by order of President Polk (with Brigham Young's approval). It initially numbered about 500 men.

Many of the men mustered out of the Battalion went to Utah where Mormon Salt Lake City was beginning to rise on the salt flats. Others drifted around California.

January, 1848, found six veterans of the Mormon Battalion in Northern California building a sawmill for a local landowner named John Augustus Sutter. One morning, the mill supervisor, James Marshall, looked down into the swirling water of the millrace and noticed a glittering piece of metal. Picking it up, he turned it over in his hand.

That evening, Mormon Henry Bigler made a note in his diary: "This day some kind of metal was found in the millrace . . . looks like gold."

Mr. Horton Builds a City

7

The Gold Rush of 1849 swept California like a grass fire. Madness was in the air. Farmers left their plows, teachers left their schoolrooms and the mudflats of San Francisco were littered with ships abandoned in favor of the mines. Soldiers left their posts; at Monterey, the entire garrison deserted. The 164-man crew of the warship U.S.S. *Warren* deserted in a matter of hours. Commodore Thomas ap Catesby Jones offered a reward of $40,000 for their return and reported, "For the present, and I fear for years to come, it will be impossible for the United States to maintain any naval or military establishment in California."

In his book *Early Recollections of the Mines*, James Carson captured the gold lust in words: "A frenzy seized my soul; I was soon in the street in search of necessary outfits; piles of gold rose up before me at every step; thousands of slaves bowed to my beck and call; myriads of fair virgins contended for my love; [these] were among the fancies of my fevered imagination. The Rothschilds, Giards, and Astors appeared to me but poor people; in short, I had a very violent attack of gold fever."

Meanwhile: In the dusty collection of buildings called San Diego, gold was only a rumor. The great gold mines of Julian lay years in the future, and placer mining along the streams of the water-rich north was a luxury the arid south could not offer.

Quite a few San Diegans did go north to the gold fields. A young Canadian miner named William Perkins wrote in his diary of "Lorenzo Soto, of San Diego [who] . . . worked about eight days on his claim, and from the amount of gold I saw and from what he told me it weighed, he had taken out 52 pounds. The claim had reached water, and in this condition he sold it to some Machados from San Diego, who also took considerable gold from it."

Opposite page
City Builder: Thirty years after this picture was taken, Alonzo Horton happened to attend a San Francisco lecture in which San Diego was praised.

Unlike Lorenzo Soto and the "Machados from San Diego," many gold hunters found only hard work and harder times. For some, golden dreams led to lonely graves. Late in 1849, a miner noted in his journal, "One young man near us has just died. He was without companion or friend, alone in his tent. Not even his name could be discovered. We buried him, tied down his tent, leaving his effects within."

Davis' Folly: The San Diego of 1850 consisted of a few haphazard wooden buildings and an occasional crumbling adobe. In the center of town was a dreary, bare earth plaza. On nearby Presidio Hill, the fortress that once marked an outpost of Imperial Spain had been worn away to a few mounds of earth.

But two men had a far-sighted plan for the town. William Hearth "Kanaka Bill" Davis, a former ship's captain who had become a wealthy financier, and a government surveyor named Andrew Gray were certain San Diego could one day become a great seaport. Once the town itself was moved from the foot of Presidio Hill to the harbor's edge, wharves and warehouses could be built to receive lucrative cargo. In time, San Diego might even rival San Francisco as the Queen City of the Pacific Coast.

Others joined Davis and Gray in their ambitious plans. William Ferrell, a lawyer who would later become San Diego's district attorney, and Californios like Miguel de Pedrorena and Jose Antonio Aguirre were especially enthusiastic.

In March, 1850, the partners paid $2304 for 160 acres of bayfront land. Fifty-six blocks were neatly laid out, wells were dug, a warehouse went up, and a wharf was built. The U.S. Army built a supply depot, and 14 prefabricated houses, shipped from Maine, were unloaded and assembled. It appeared the dream was rapidly becoming reality.

But in late March, 1851, Miguel de Pedrorena died suddenly of apoplexy. And the army, which had plans to build in Davis' "New Town," had second thoughts. The federal government decided against building either a customs house or a post office in the infant settlement. Many San Diegans, preferring the dusty streets of Old Town, simply refused to have anything to do with the idea. In the saloons it was laughingly called "Davis' Folly." And when a San Francisco fire left Davis with $700,000 in losses, he announced that he would no longer be able to underwrite New Town. Within a few years, all that remained of "Davis' Folly" were occasional lonely buildings on the mudflat with the wind whistling through their broken windows. That and a few bored soldiers sitting in the sun outside the supply depot, watching seagulls pluck fish from the bay.

In 1861, soldiers from the depot tore down Davis' wharf for firewood. Davis presented a bill for $60,000 to the Federal Government, which finally paid him $6,000 in 1885.

Davis and Gray were men ahead of their time, a fact even Davis admitted. When he visited San Diego in 1887, he said of his earlier plans, "At that time I predicted that San Diego would become a great commercial seaport from its fine geographic position and from the fact that it was the only good harbor south of San Francisco. Had it not been for our Civil War, railroads would have reached here years before Stanford's road was built, and our wharf was ready for business."

A little less than a century after Davis' 1887 visit, only one of his pre-fabricated houses remained near the bay, on 11th Avenue in the warehouse district. But in early March, 1984, it was moved several blocks away to become the headquarters of the San Diego Gaslamp Quarter Council.

Another Davis legacy is Pantoja Park, bounded by G, F, Columbia, and India streets downtown. Davis had intended the park to be New Town's plaza. Today the block is surrounded by luxury condominiums.

Statehood: On September 9, 1850, California became a state, the union's 31st. State or not, however, it was still in many ways a rough frontier. In his Inaugural Address, first governor Peter Burnett pointed out that "The discovery of the rich . . . . gold mines of California produced a singular state of things in this community, unparalleled, perhaps, in the annals of mankind. We have here in our midst, a mixed mass of human beings from every part of the wide earth, of different habits, manners, customs and opinions, all, however, impelled onward by the same feverish desire of fortune-making . . . the state of our government is still more unprecedented and alarming. We are in fact without government . . . a commercial, civilized and wealthy people, without law order or system."

Governor Burnett, like just about everyone else in the new state, was a gold seeker.

Around San Diego, law and order was a fragile institution, brutal at times, neglectful at others. A man could be hung for as little as stealing a row boat. Cattle and horse thieves roamed the back country while stabbings, shootings, and brawls were distressingly common.

Prosperity, flowering up north in the gold country, continued to elude San Diego. In mid-1850, it became a city with a mayor and city council; a year later, the city was bankrupt and ordered by the state to sell off civic property to pay its bills. The brand-new San Diego *Herald* moaned in late 1851, "We are obliged to send to San Francisco for everything we eat except fresh beef and garlic."

One San Diego jail was built so poorly that a prisoner dug his way out with a pocket knife—and escaped.

San Diego also continued to be isolated by geography. Ships usually ignored the port as they steamed or sailed north to San Francisco. To the east lay mountains and desert. In San Diego, writer Bayard Taylor reported, "The emigrants by the Gila route gave a terrible account of the crossing of the Great desert, lying west of the Colorado. They described this region as scorching and sterile, a country of burning salt plains and shifting hills of sand, whose only signs of human visitation are the bones of animals and men . . . There, if a man faltered, he was gone; no one could stop to lend him a hand without a likelihood of sharing his fate."

The years following the U.S. occupation brought sorrow and poverty to the Californios as the American flood destroyed their pastoral way of life. Mariano Vallejo wrote bitterly, "I assert that . . . the North Americans have treated the Californians as a conquered people and not as citizens who voluntarily joined to form part of the great family dwelling beneath the glorious flag which flamed so proudly from Bunker Hill."

Vallejo, son of the influential soldier Ignacio Vallejo, was important not only as a general and a statesman, but also as northern Sonoma County's first vintner.

The Last Warriors: The Californios became a displaced people under the Americans, but the Indians fared far worse. Emigrant John Doble noted in his diary, "An Indian was shot for stealing by some emigrants up the road nine or ten miles yesterday which has created a little stir among the Indians, but not of any consequence."

When, in late 1850, the city decided to levy a tax on Indians to bolster a dwindling treasury, some, like Antonio Garra, could bear the oppression no longer.

On November 27, 1851, Warner's Ranch, near Garra's home, was attacked by 100 warriors. Three miles away, Indians surprised a group of tourists at a hot springs and killed four. For a brief time, San Diego, in a panic, was placed under martial law. In a letter to his mother, an excited Thomas Whaley wrote, "We momentarily expect to be attacked by the Indians who under their great chief Antonio Garra are swarming by the thousands."

In the end, the "thousands" of Indians did not materialize, and the pathetic revolt was swiftly broken. Asked to attend a peace conference, Garra was instead arrested. In January, 1852, he stood by an open grave before a firing squad. With great dignity he made a brief statement: "Gentlemen, I ask your pardon for all my offenses, and expect yours in return." A few moments later, the sound of gunfire echoed across Old Town.

Cattle Baron: The ferocious-looking Cave Couts became a wealthy rancher following his Army career.

A Distant War: In April, 1861, the telegraph line brought ominous news. In Charleston, South Carolina, Confederate gunners had opened fire on Fort Sumter, and the Civil War had begun. Riders rode south from Los Angeles to San Diego with the latest dispatches. The town quickly found itself split into two angry camps. Pro-southerners included Virginia-born County Clerk George Pendleton and Tennesseean Cave Couts, who owned the prosperous Guajome Rancho. Among those favoring the Union cause were most of Old Town's merchants, including Ephraim Morse

and Robert Israel. Governor Peter Burnett tried to prevent all free blacks from entering California (as he had done previously in Oregon). In the 1850s, slaves were advertised in the Sacramento papers. One ad offered a "$300" male slave for $100 if the buyer would then free the slave. The seller stated he was making "this great sacrifice in the value of the property, to satisfy myself whether they prefer to pay a small sum to release him, or play their old game and try and steal him."

Old Town: The dusty little burg was a long way from becoming the metropolis some visionaries imagined.

After the war broke out, Union troops arrived in San Diego and arrested several Confederate sympathizers, including some suspected of being members of the secret pro-southern "Knights of the Golden Circle." Still, some San Diegans remained southern to the core. George Pendleton, who graduated from West Point with future generals Grant and Sherman, wrote to rancher Cave Couts in 1863, "I have all those fellows here spotted who voted the Black Republican ticket . . ."

Racial discrimination did not end with the Civil War. In 1865, New England-bred schoolteacher Mary Walker was seen having lunch with a black lady friend. She was promptly fired. "You see," sniffed a San Diegan to a San Francisco newspaper, "we are a high-toned people down here . . . and we don't intend to tolerate anything of this kind."

"Black Republican" was a derogatory term for a republican who favored abolition. They were also, according to one southern Democrat, "Radicals, prohibitionists, free lovers and cigar-smoking women."

But Mary Walker had not been impressed with what she found upon her arrival in San Diego in April, 1865:

Schoolmarm: Mary Walker dedicated herself to San Diego despite its "dilapidated" air. In November, 1976, the Mary Chase Walker Elementary School was dedicated in Mira Mesa.

Sarah Babe Horton may have been Alonzo Horton's third or possibly fifth wife, depending on the account. Despite several marriages, Horton had no children.

It was a most desolate looking landscape. The hills were brown and barren; not a tree or green thing was to be seen. Of all the dilapidated, miserable looking places I had ever seen this was the worst. The first night of my stay at the hotel a donkey came under my window and saluted me with an unearthly bray. The fleas were plentiful and hungry. Mosquitoes were also in attendance. My school was composed mostly of Spanish and halfbreed children and several Americans. At recess the Spanish girls smoked cigaritas and the boys amused themselves by lassoing pigs, hens, etc.

But the winds of change were preparing to blow hard on San Diego, however. Two years later in San Francisco, a lecture was offered on "The Ports of the Pacific Coast," and called San Diego, "One of the healthiest places in the world with one of the best harbors as well." The lecture was a success but one man in the audience seemed particularly impressed. Alonzo Horton thought about it all the way home, and just couldn't get San Diego out of his mind.

Quite Logical: Sarah Babe Horton wasn't really surprised when her husband Alonzo crawled out of bed at two a.m. to sit in the living room peering at a map. In the six years she had been married to this human dynamo, she had come to accept the fact that Alonzo was often restless. But she was a bit startled when he announced brightly, "I am going to sell my goods and go to San Diego and build a city." Horton recalled that his wife "said I talked like a wild man."

Even so she wasn't too worried. Alonzo had come home from the previous night's lecture fascinated, but it would pass. She knew it would take at least six months to sell off their furniture store stock. By that time, Alonzo would be sure to have lost interest in his latest enthusiasm. But Horton sold off everything in three days. It was, he happily explained, "Not an auction sale but just a run of business which seemed providential."

At that, Sarah threw up her hands and went off to pack her china. To Horton it all seemed quite logical. "My wife said she would not oppose me any longer, for she had always noticed when it was right for me to do anything, it always went right in my favor."

One Dollar Pig: Alonzo Erastus Horton was born in Union, Connecticut, in 1813. Eight years later he made his first major purchase: a pig for one dollar. About 70 years later, he was still buying and selling. At various times in his life, he worked as a grocer, lumberjack, schoolteacher, and constable. He traded in wheat, cattle, ice, gold dust, furni-

ture, real estate, and just about anything else a person might buy. He made barrels and baskets, sawed timber, sailed the Great Lakes, and dug for gold in two countries. He carried the mail as an express rider. Horton was trusted and well-liked in his business dealings; his credo was "To be as happy as I can every day; to try to make everyone else as happy as I can, and to try to make no one unhappy."

In 1847, Horton went to Wisconsin and bought 1500 acres of forest for 70 cents apiece. He built a saw mill and a steamer landing on a nearby river, then began to lay out a small town which he cheerfully named "Hortonville." Before long, modest homes and stores sprang up as settlers moved into Mr. Horton's village (built with timber from Mr. Horton's mill). After almost five years, the restless Horton sold out for $7,000 and went off to join the Gold Rush. Once in California, it didn't take Horton long to figure out that there was more money in the buying and selling of gold than in digging for it. By 1856, he was quite well off and ready to return east. The following year he boarded the Panama-bound *Cortez* on the first leg of the long journey. He brought $10,000 in gold dust in his baggage and another $5,000 in a money belt.

New Town: Horton's New Town moved San Diego to where it belonged—the shores of San Diego Bay.

Horton built a profitable Gold Rush business bringing ice from the mountains to the towns. In a relatively short time, he made $8,000, which was more than most Forty-Niners made mining.

Mr. Horton Builds a City

Disaster waited in Panama. While in a hotel, Horton and his fellow passengers were besieged by a mob. During the melee, Horton opened fire with a pistol. A few minutes later, the mob fell back, leaving behind eight dead. Horton led the passengers to safety on the *Cortez*. But he was forced to leave his baggage (and his $10,000) behind.

In the east, Horton fell in love with Sarah Wilson Babe, whom he called "Babe," and married her in June, 1860. That year Horton went to Washington to present claims concerning the Panamanian riot. There he was noticed by Secretary of State William Henry Seward, who offered him a job in the State Department. Horton thanked him, but went off instead to prospect in the icy mountains of British Columbia. Finally, in 1862, he and Babe returned to San Francisco and opened a furniture business. At last Horton seemed to have settled down. But then came the lecture on Pacific ports, and Alonzo Horton was on the move again.

I t Doesn't Lie Right!": On April 15, 1867, Horton came down the gangplank of the steamer *Pacific* to a ramshackle San Diego dock. A wagon brought him up a rutted road to the dirt streets of Old Town. The grubby little group of buildings didn't look very promising as a future metropolis. As a matter of fact, about the only thing that seemed to prosper in San Diego were the fleas, which infested everyone and everything.

It took disembarking ship passengers a half hour to reach the inland village.

A Wells Fargo agent who had been on the *Pacific* with Horton asked how he liked the town. "I would not give you five dollars for the whole of it," Horton growled. "I would not take it as a gift! It doesn't lie right! Never in the world can you have a city here."

Instead, he announced, San Diego ought to be closer to the bay. He was already laying out the streets and lots of a new San Diego in his mind. Years later he recalled the bayfront just "seemed to be the best spot for building a city that I ever saw."

In his enthusiasm to build his new city, Horton faced one problem immediately. The land was publicly owned and an election was required before it could be sold. Horton quickly sought out the county clerk and plunked down ten dollars to pay for the election. That taken care of, he looked for a hotel room. Thus ended Alonzo Horton's first day in San Diego.

A few days later Horton paid a visit to the town's one-room schoolhouse. There he delivered a cheerful speech to teacher August Barrett's class. "My young friends! It will take young ideas to make your city great. Your old fogies think I am crazy because I plan to build a city on your mesa . . . They are shortsighted cynics, who would only look down the tips of their sunburned noses."

Opposite page
New Town: Horton used this map to lure buyers to what was still largely mudflat and sagebrush.

A Short History of San Diego

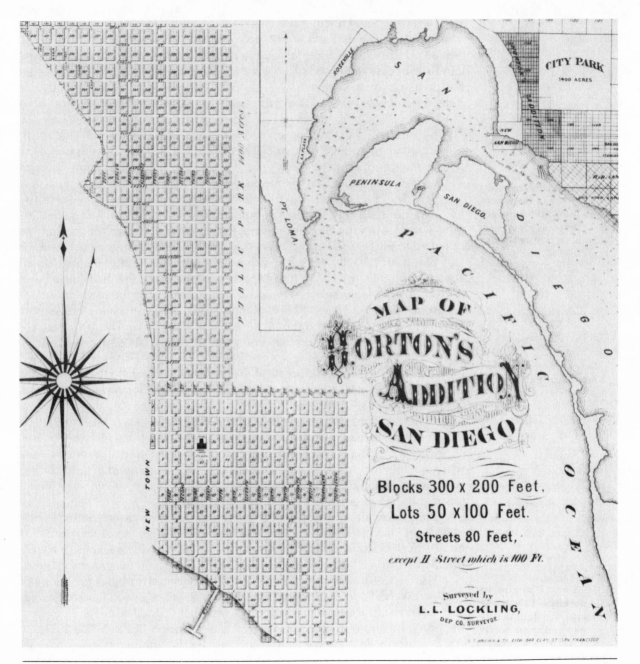

Selling San Diego: A little less than a month later the land auction was held. The first lot to come up consisted of 200 acres. Horton bid $100. There was a ripple of laughter in the crowd. "I thought they were laughing because I bid so little," remembered Horton, "but on inquiring what it was customary to pay for land, I was told that twenty dollars was a good price if the land was smooth, or about fifteen dollars if it was rough. I did not bid so much after that."

By that evening, Horton owned 960 acres of mudflats and sagebrush, purchased at an average price of 27½ cents an acre. Most locals considered the whole affair a grand joke. But a few, including influential merchant Ephraim Morse, were thinking that just maybe Horton was on to something.

Still, the memory of "Davis' Folly" was fresh. But unlike Davis, Horton had experience in this business of building towns, and was a first-rate sales-man with a carefully thought-out marketing strategy. After the auction, he returned to San Francisco and opened a sales office on Montgomery Street.

One man who did buy a lot (with a money-back guarantee if not satisfied) was Sammuel Dunnels. On his property was one of the few remaining Davis houses. Dunnels remade the building into a hotel, then he took out an ad-vertisement in the *Union*: "This splendid and new First Class Hotel is now open. New furniture throughout. All persons visiting San Diego in search of health, recreation or pleasure will find good accommodations at this House. It is pleasantly situated near the steamer landing. The table is constantly supplied with the best the market affords and every attention is paid to the comfort and convenience of guests." It wasn't long before Dunnels' hotel was doing a brisk business.

In his San Francisco sales office, Horton spread his maps often for poten-tial buyers. He had plenty of corner lots available for merchants (he had shrewdly made the blocks shorter so there would be plenty of corners). There were free lots for churches, and for home buyers, he promised to throw in free whitewash (enough to cover the two sides of the house visible to incoming steamship passengers). Business picked up rapidly.

The *Union*, in its eight years of existence, had never seen anything quite like Horton's New Town San Diego. In November, 1868, the paper noted, "At New Town, buildings are in the process of creation in all directions. We were told Mr. Horton is selling from $600 to $1000 worth of lots every day."

Horton returned from San Francisco and began to build on his own. Horton's Wharf soon poked out into the bay, Horton's Bank Block followed, and after that, the luxurious Horton House Hotel opened its doors. In front of his hotel, he laid out what today is still called Horton Plaza. In late 1869, the *Union* announced, "People are coming here by the hundreds, by steamer, by

Horton usually carried his New Town, San Diego maps in a musician's horn case. San Franciscans began pointing him out as "that crazy man with a tin horn."

Many of Horton's first lots were actually given away.

Horton House cost its developer $150,000; he managed to furnish it by paying on time, nearly unheard of in those days.

A Short History of San Diego

stage and by private conveyance . . . From a place of no importance . . . we now have a city of 3,000 inhabitants . . . Every steamer from San Francisco averages 200 passengers for San Diego."

Young in Heart: The years would bring business successes and reverses for Horton. They would also bring sorrow, as when his beloved Babe was killed in a carriage accident in 1889. When he remarried two years later, the *Union* reported that the groom "is thirty years senior of the bride, but is young in heart and certain he will live to see San Diego as the metropolis of the coast."

An 1888 book, *The City and County of San Diego*, paid homage to Horton:

> It was the boast of Augustus Caesar that he found Rome in brick and he should leave it in marble. With more regard to truth might Alonzo E. Horton, speaking in the figurative style adopted by the Roman Emperor, remark that he found San Diego a barren waste, and today, as he looks down from the portico of his beautiful mansion on Florence Heights, he sees it a busy, thriving city of 35,000 inhabitants. Probably there is no other instance in the history of our country, where great cities have grown from insignificant beginnings, where the presence of one man, unaided by abundant capital, has accomplished such wonderful results as have been achieved by A.E. Horton in San Diego.

In 1895, the city of San Diego purchased Horton plaza from him for $10,000, payable at $100 a month. Since Horton was 81, it was not expected that the full amount would have to be paid. But Horton lived until January, 1909, far beyond the receipt of his last payment.

But in 1869 such homage lay far in the future. And even as Horton was unrolling his maps, new forces were about to shape San Diego's destiny. In the mountains near what is now the town of Julian, rancher Fred Coleman stopped at a stream to let his horse drink. There had been little rain in the winter of 1869 and the water was only a trickle. Coleman saw some small stones glitter, and he reached into the cold water to grasp them.

The Gold Rush was about to come to San Diego.

Bad Men, Good Men

8

In the time between Alonzo Horton's arrival and the discovery of gold, San Diego swelled from a grubby handful of buildings into a neat, prosperous city. In the years since statehood, it had sometimes seemed that the town's future lay in being the butt of a series of saloon jokes. An early book recorded one typical story: "You pick up a handful of dirt and in two seconds half of it is gone. That's fleas. In a minute more the rest has slipped through your fingers. That's sand. That's where it gets its name from, Sa-a-a-ndy Ago!" A variation reported that the name actually was "Sandyague, from sand and ague [fever]," which were supposed to be the leading features "next to rattlesnakes and tarantulas."

But by the early 1870s, the laughter was stopping. The city began to spread out, filling in the blank spaces on Horton's maps. Many newcomers came by steamer around Cape Horn or down from San Francisco, and tied up to the docks that now pushed out into the bay. Or they arrived by stage coach across dreary deserts from the east. They were builders and dreamers, card-sharps, hustlers and con men, gamblers, gunfighters, farmers, school teachers, and cattlemen. New Bedford whaling men arrived to hunt gray whales in San Diego Bay. Hard rock miners came down from the northern mines to blast and dig the gold from San Diego's mountains. The exotic sounds of China were heard on the waterfront streets as Cantonese merchants opened their shops.

But in April, 1872, misfortune struck: fire roared through the heart of Old Town, destroying much of San Diego's original business district. The fire dashed the hopes of those who were certain Old Town would prevail over the "new" San Diego. Saving what they could, merchants abandoned Old Town, and moved to the growing Americanized city on the waterfront. Already the pastoral Spanish and Mexican past was taking on the romantic glow of history.

Opposite page
Busted: This 1888 photograph was theatrical all right, but no one looks tempted to smile.

Fires like the one that ravaged Old Town in 1872 were a common scourge of 19th century cities. In San Diego's Gaslamp Quarter, fire-resistant brick walls and metal shutters can still be found.

Scientist William Brewer noted in his diary, "I find it hard to realize I am in America, in the United States, the young vigorous republic as we call her, when I see these [mission] ruins. They carry me back again to the Old World with its decline and decay, with its histories of war and blood and strife and desolation . . ."

Gold: One of the biggest spurs to the town's growth was the discovery of gold. The hunch that there was gold in the mountains east of San Diego was an old one. As early as 1602, Father Antonio de la Asunción reported that in San Diego's beach sand there was a "great quantity of yellow pyrites all full of holes, a sure sign that in the mountains . . . there are gold mines, for the water, when it rains, brings it down from the mountains."

In 1849, almost two and half centuries later, Army engineer C.C. Parry reported that along Banner Canyon "we have an approach to the gold formation, and in the section of the country just limited, exist the fairest prospects of mineral discoveries."

By the winter of 1870, the hunch shared by an army engineer and a Spanish priest had blossomed into a roaring gold rush. Fred Coleman started it with his chance discovery, and before long miners were prospecting 50 miles away in all directions. At first, miners simply dipped their pans into the swirling waters of creeks and streams fat with snow melt and sifted out bits of gold. But within a few months, gold became scarce, and streams faded into dust in the summer heat. The major deposits lay deep in the earth, and could only be reached through shafts. Many of the mines were ramshackle affairs, glory holes that put out pay dirt for a while and then died. Some are remembered for their whimsical names: Jolly Boy, Shoo Fly, Don't Bother Me, You Bet, Red Rooster. Others are remembered for their wealth: Washington, General McClellan, and the mighty Stonewall Jackson, so rich it shunned Wells Fargo and ran its own gold shipments.

Two mine shafts that can still be seen are the Stonewall Jackson, now fenced off as part of Cuyamaca Rancho State Park, and the Eagle, near Julian, which is privately-owned and features a museum and guided tours.

Typical of the great mines was the Helvetia. One awed newspaper reporter wrote, "Not enough could be said about the continued fabulous richness of the Helvetia ledge. It is no word painting or stretch of the truth to say that some of this quartz is literally stuck together and hinged with gold, and this is not in mere isolated pieces or specimen rock, but great chunks of ore coming up with each bucket are scored and seamed, flaked and spotted with the precious metal."

Throughout the early 1870s, such mines yielded hundreds of thousands of dollars. The Stonewall Jackson produced two million dollars in gold, the Owens came in with $450,000. Almost a mile west of the town of Julian, the

Julian: San Diego's Gold Rush came late but lucratively.

Eagle and High Peak mines dug into "Gold Hill" and produced almost $100,000 between them.

Roulette Wheels: Rude gold camps sprang up near the mines, ramshackle wood and canvas towns where a saloon might be little more than a board across two barrels and a few bottles of whiskey. Most of them died when the mines closed. Today they are only names on maps sold to tourists: Emily City, Rag Town, Branson, and Cuyamaca City, for example. A few, like Banner, hung on after the mines closed. In 1894, the Julian *Sentinel* reported, "Fortunes of Banner boomed, faded, then boomed again. By 1892, twenty years later, it was again a thriving back country metropolis. It had a school of thirty students, all grades from primary through high . . . Banner's graduating class equalled that of National City and exceeded Escondido." Today, though, even the foundations of Banner's buildings are lost in the chaparral.

By 1874, the Gold Rush was over in San Diego. The veins of the San Diego mines were fractured, torn and splintered by ancient geologic upheavals. The shining metal danced in and out of the rock, at times teasingly close, at other times heartbreakingly distant. One by one, the mines "winked out" and closed. With them, the gold towns collapsed, leaving behind only their dead in overgrown and long-forgotten boot hills.

One town that has survived is Julian, 60 miles from San Diego in the Cuyamaca Mountains. The town was founded in 1869 by four ex-Confederate soldiers, Drew and James Bailey and their cousins, Webb and Mike Julian. The town flourished during the Gold Rush. In the late 1880s, two freed slaves, Albert and Margaret Robinson, built a gracious hotel there with a loan from a Major Chase, who was Alfred's ex-master. Today, the Julian Hotel still looks out over the Main Street. The guests are mainly tourists who flock to Julian in increasing numbers to savor a little of San Diego's Gold rush past. Other visitors come to Julian to savor its clean mountain air or play in the snow that blankets the area in the winter.

From New Bedford and Nantucket: Gold wasn't the only source of natural wealth in and around San Diego. For uncounted centuries migrating gray whales had come to San Diego to calve. The Indians, lacking the tools to hunt the whales, left them unmolested and they held little interest for the Spanish and Mexicans. But the cycle was broken in the 1850s when American whalers arrived from the docks of New Bedford and Nantucket.

As the huge beasts slid into San Diego Bay, the whalers put out in small boats with their harpoons ready. People came to watch from bluffs overlooking the water. Spotting a cow fat with blubber, the whalers would make their kill.

City by the Bay: In the 1870s and 1880s, San Diego began edging along the bay. Old Town, with its dusty streets and adobe buildings, was slipping into history.

Then the massive carcass would be towed to Ballast Point and hauled up on the beach. There it was sliced into thick pieces to be rendered into oil. A heavy, foul smoke would drift across the bay as clouds of sea gulls wheeled above the remains.

Few whales were taken at first. In 1859, the *Herald* reported, "The company of whalemen . . . have killed about a dozen whales in the few weeks since they have commenced operations, only five of which they have been able to get into port. These five yielded 150 barrels of oil, worth about $2,000. If some means could be devised to prevent the whales from sinking, three or four parties could do a good business during the season, by catching whales within ten miles of the entrance to the harbor."

By the winter of 1871, improved technology and a healthy market made whaling a big business in San Diego. That season, 55,000 gallons of whale oil were taken. But as the hunt continued, the whales began to avoid San Diego Bay. Not long after, in search of new hunting grounds, the whalers also left San Diego.

Boom and Bust: To a casual observer, San Diego in the early 1870s was a prosperous, bustling city. But a closer look would have revealed the fragile underpinnings of that prosperity. The mines were still churning out wealth, and the real estate business was moving along briskly (some said it moved a little *too* briskly). But if prosperity was to continue, a long-term economic base was needed.

Now protected by mutual agreement between Canada, Mexico, and the United States, the gray whale herds have begun to grow slowly. Along California's coast, winter whale-watching trips from small boats are very popular.

"Metropolis of Southern California": San Diego's climate is so mild the caption for this engraving said, "even in January and February . . . a child might play on the seashore without suffering the slightest inconvenience."

That base was slow in building, and the city began to ride a roller coaster of boom and bust. Paper empires, built on the shifting sands of hopes and vague promises, rose and fell. By 1874, the gold mining frenzy had sputtered out. About the same time, the bottom fell out of the whaling business as the gray whales sought safer sanctuaries in Baja California lagoons. Heavy industry lay far in the future, and tourism was in its infancy. There was agriculture of course; the cattle ranches and orchards of San Diego were well established. But there was always the threat of drought which could decimate herds and shrivel crops.

The city's move to New Town was complicated by suits and countersuits. The issue was finally resolved by the California Supreme Court in favor of the movers.

In search of an ecomomic panacea, San Diego's citizens hungered for a railroad. If the city were tied to the rest of the country by rail, whole new markets would open up for local products. In early 1871, it was announced that the Texas and Pacific Line would be built linking San Diego with the east via Texas. The city prepared for a glowing future. The weekly *Union* became a daily. In Old Town, the board of supervisors packed up the city records and moved them into Horton's bustling New Town. On August 12, 1871, the corner stone was laid for the new court house, and on October 12, the city treated itself to a shiny new fire engine.

But two years later, the railroad still had not come. In fact, it didn't look as if it ever would. Depression settled over the city. The following year, 1874, brought more gloomy news. The War Department, which had been building a fort on Ballast Point, announced that because of budget cuts, work on the fort would stop. (More than two decades would pass before building was resumed.) The Chamber of Commerce tried to strike a cheerful note with a new pamphlet touting San Diego's healing climate: "As a national sanitarium, San Diego is unsurpassed. Hundreds of invalids have been restored to health, or greatly benefited, by our health-giving climate." But the *Union* continued to print the economic casualty lists of foreclosure sales, and the mood remained gloomy. The city's population fell from four to two thousand, as people loaded their goods into wagons and rumbled out of town in search of greener pastures.

Charles Crocker was not the only mogul to scorn San Diego. Fellow railroad tycoon Collis Huntington said that as far as he was concerned, "Grass could grow in [its] streets." Phineas Banning, dredging a harbor north of Long Beach, tossed 50 cents to a friend and told him to buy Horton's New Town and keep the change.

In 1876, the powerful Southern Pacific Railroad began laying track into Los Angeles. San Diegans pleaded their case for having the line extended south from Los Angeles but to no avail. As far as the Southern Pacific was concerned, San Diego was expendable. "You will never live long enough," growled railroad magnate Charles Crocker, "to see a railroad laid to the Bay of San Diego, nor one laid in the state by a transcontinental railroad which we do not lay . . . I have my foot on the neck of San Diego and I'm going to keep it there."

But Crocker did not count on the perseverance of the San Diegans and the ambitions of the rival Santa Fe Railroad. Less than a decade later, in 1885, the first Santa Fe train from the east puffed into San Diego. It was greeted by a

A Short History of San Diego

Grand Hotel: Across the bay from San Diego the elaborate red-roofed Del Coronado was taking shape.

pelting rain and about 100 bedraggled but enthusiastic welcomers.

The Santa Fe eastern link would exist only six years. In 1891, winter flash floods rolled down Temecula Canyon and washed out the railroad tracks. The Santa Fe decided not to rebuild and San Diego was again, except for a spur line to Los Angeles, cut off. The city was left with a splendid railroad depot and no where to go.

Mundane Business: Despite the cycles of fortune, the mundane business of building a city continued throughout the 1880s. In 1886, San Diego's first electric street lights cast their glow over newly-graded streets. Trolley lines were laid down and by 1888, the city had 37 miles of trolley tracks. Telephone poles rose along the streets as a web of wires was spun across the skyline. Down Fifth Avenue, in what is now the heart of the Gaslamp Quarter, a series of elegant office buildings rose. On the bay, a stub-nosed ferry began huffing its way between Coronado and San Diego. Outside town, suburbs began to dot the map. From La Jolla in the north to South San Diego Beach and Oneonta in the south, speculators laid out streets for new towns. By 1890, San Diego's population had passed 16,000.

On Coronado Island, long the domain of ground squirrels and rattlesnakes, Elisha Babcock and H.L. Story were building a gingerbread castle amid the sage. Workmen, from master carpenters to Chinese laborers, lived on the

For a few weeks in July, 1886, the steam yacht *Della* served as a ferry. But in August, the *Coronado* began regular service as the first "true" ferry on the bay. In 1924, the *Coronado*, decked out as a Spanish galleon, was exploded and sunk for the movie *Captain Blood*.

Because Coronado Island was so bare, virtually everything used in the construction of the Hotel Del Coronado had to be brought to the site, including fresh water, which was (and still is) piped under the bay from San Diego.

site in tents. Ground was broken in early 1887 and, soon after, a huge and spindly skeleton of timber could be seen across the bay from San Diego. Construction proceeded rapidly and by December, 1887, the crisp white walls and red roofs of the Hotel Del Coronado were in place. In February, 1888, one year and a million dollars (a huge sum for the time) after groundbreaking, the hotel was open for business. The first register, stiff in its new bindings, was opened, and wealthy rancher Nelson Morris signed for a suite of nine rooms. On its front page, the *Union* pronounced the Del Coronado, "A Hotel That is Surpassed by None in the World, Like Unto an Old Norman Castle."

The 1880s also saw the growth of culture and new ideas in San Diego. Renowned writer and musician Jesse Shepard entertained frequently in his "Villa Montezuma" (now beautifully restored and the pride of the San Diego Historical Society). Visiting writer Helen Hunt Jackson gathered material for her romantic novel *Ramona*. "I am going to write a novel," she wrote to a friend in 1883, "in which will be set forth some Indian experiences in a way to move people's hearts . . . If I can do one hundredth part for the Indians as Mrs. Stowe did for the Negroes, I will be grateful."

Meanwhile, south of San Diego on a hill not far from the Mexican border, John J. Montgomery was experimenting with human flight. In August, 1883, a glider with Montgomery at the controls was pulled down the hill. A moment later the glider swooped 600 feet into the summer air in the first controlled flight in a heavier-than-air machine. Two decades later, the Wright Brothers would lift off the sands of Kitty Hawk in the first airplane. What is often forgotten is that much of their research was based on principles first realized by John Montgomery.

Jesse Shepard: Spiritualist, pianist, bon vivant. When he moved to San Diego, the citizenry was thrilled: Culture had arrived.

Stingaree: With her proud new big-city look, San Diego began to find herself with big-city woes. One of the worst of these was a raunchy, hell-raising part of town called the Stingaree. On the waterfront between First and Fifth Avenues, the Stingaree was several square blocks of bawdy houses, gin joints, gambling halls, and opium dens that folded during the day and blossomed at night like dark flowers.

Sailors reeled in and out of saloons with names like the "Seven Buckets of Blood," "The Pacific Squadron," and "One-Eyed" McInery's. At Till A. Barnes' place, drinkers gawked at Barnes' pet bear chained outside. Or they might gamble at one of the Stingaree's dozens of gambling joints, including three owned by cold-eyed Wyatt Earp. Earp liked San Diego; in any case it was a lot more friendly than Arizona, where they were asking unpleasant questions about the recent shootout at the OK Corral.

The Stingaree was also home for most of San Diego's growing Chinese population. Most of the Chinese, like the respected merchants Ah Quin and Wo Sing, whose fishing junks dotted the bay, led quiet lives as they made their way in the land they called the "Golden Hills." As gold miner William Kelley observed, the Chinese "are quick, industrious and perservering; they are systematic, sober and cleanly . . . They, above all others, appear successful in finding employment; for you never see a Chinese lolling about, or amongst the group of idlers."

Unfortunately, Chinatown's exoticness and its inhabitants' success at finding employment gave rise to ill-feeling on the part of many Californians, especially during hard economic times. For many decades, the state's Chinese immigrants were subjected to abuse, both unthinking and malicious.

Not all who plagued the Chinese were *fan kwei* (foreign devils). There were times when they were victimized by racketeering "tongs." Narcotics in San Diego were a lucrative business, with opium dens bluntly listed in the city directory. And Chinatown was still a place where "young women, bought on a Chinese dock and shipped to America as slaves, were kept in prostitute's cribs."

One such unfortunate was Ling Yee, who was left in San Diego as security on a debt. Ah Quock, the George Marston family's cook, saw her and fell in love; he paid the debt and married her. But soon after, she was kidnapped by tong warriors and taken to Los Angeles. George W. Marston quickly made the trip north, found, and freed Ling Yee.

On July 18, 1873, the *Union* happily reported, "Mr. George W. Marston arrived on the *Mohongo* yesterday, bringing back with him Ling Yee, the Chinese woman whose attempted abduction by the Chinese in Los Angeles has heretofor been noticed at length. The poor creature was overjoyed at being returned to her husband, home and kind friends. Mr. G.P. Marston and his son George W. Marston, deserve the warmest commendation for the earnest and generous [efforts] put forth to save this persecuted woman."

"John Chinaman": California's Chinese were subjected to every kind of abuse, but most managed to lead quiet, industrious lives.

The word "tong" means "association" and most tongs are simply business or social organizations. Some criminal tongs, though, became extremely powerful.

Wobblies, Cultists, and Flying Fools

9

In the early 1880s, San Diego real estate was being bought and sold almost as rapidly as maps could be drawn up. But while the realtors were pitching tent offices on barren lots, other Californians were striking a glummer note. In Wallace Elliott's 1883 *History of San Bernardino and San Diego Counties*, T.S. Van Dyke commented:

> San Diego County, as seen by about nine-tenths of those who have heretofore visited it, is anything but inviting to the settler or tourist. Hard, gravelly table-lands, either barren or clad with a dreary black brush, rolling hills of gravel bristling with cactus and cobble-stones, stony slopes scarred with gullies and washes, no trees, no streams, no springs, the general barrenness relieved only by a few choice little valleys and a few tracts of good table-land all held at high prices—such is the picture that strikes most glaringly all who approach by way of the coast.
>
> If the visitor looks inland he sees only swell after swell of bare hills looming through a dreamy haze and terminating in a high range of dark blue mountains on the East. But nowhere does his eyes [sic] rest upon anything even suggestive of farming or rural life. He returns, probably on the same steamer by which he came, fully believing that the 'nice,' 'hospitable,' and 'intelligent' people farther north who showed him such lovely orange groves and had such pretty lots to sell were nearly correct in their opinion of all of Southern California outside of their own lines. Herein the rest of Southern California has a vast advantage over San Diego.

Visiting the remains of Mission San Diego did little to improve Van Dyke's mood. He pronounced the mission grounds "a picture of dreadful dilapidation, with here and there a pile of dirt or adobe, and in other places water-chiseled columns, which seem to look down like grim mourners from their broken heights upon the scene of havoc and desolation around." When he

One imaginative ploy of San Diego's real estate peddlers was the 1889 "Ocean Beach Gold Rush" when small nuggets were "found" in the sand.

Opposite page
Airmen: Lt. T.G. Ellyon, the first naval pilot, takes the wheel of a $4000 Curtis A-1.

inspected San Diego's harbor, Van Dyke did begrudge a few words of praise. "The harbor of San Diego is large enough for all the shipping of the coast, is so land-locked and quiet that a vessel may lie at the wharf a year without marring her paint from chaffing, and is deep enough on the bar for the largest vessels to enter under full headway and in any weather."

For those foolish enough to attempt farming in San Diego, Van Dyke growled a warning. "Numerous disadvantages ... Squirrels ravage above ground; gophers below ground. The wildcat soon spies out the fatness of your hencoop; the fox and coyote are on hand almost as soon as it is built ... life is constantly enlivened by insect stimulants of all kinds. Fleas may indeed be cultivated in summer by a judicious distribution of cats and dogs over the carpets, properly reinforced by an array of swine around the kitchen door."

However, Van Dyke did have a few words of comfort for the San Diego settler, noting that "the grizzly bear [is] nearly extinct and the panther [is] too cowardly and too scarce to be considered as existing at all."

Buy La Mesa: Nay-sayers like Van Dyke were largely ignored as the boom continued to roll throughout the 1880s. As late as January, 1888, for example, the previously obscure suburb of La Mesa boasted 100 lots sold with more to come. One real estate firm couldn't resist gleeful doggerel in its February 2, 1888, ad in the San Diego *Free Press*:

La Mesa was originally called La Mesa Heights, a classic example of real estatese.

The shades of night were falling fast,
When up through San Diego passed
One hundred men whose shrewd advice,
Free given without cost or price
Was 'Buy La Mesa! Buy La Mesa!'

But a few months later the fever of speculation broke and financial depression settled over San Diego. Poverty-stricken "paper millionaires" scanned newspaper want ads and muttered that they would leave town if they could only afford it. Still, two days before Christmas, the San Diego *Bee* tried to sound a hopeful note: "The game of throwing lots back and forth ... does not necessarily mean growth, but if, after the play is over, there still looms up from the result of it material sufficiently alluring to tempt wise heads to great ventures we may be surely confident there is no danger ahead ... Southern California can't go backward. Apparently we may commit here all the follies of the calendar, and it still seems the one spot on earth where nature almost forgets to mete out to men according to their transgressions."

Hard Times: After the tumult of the Gold Rush and land speculation, the 1890s ushered in a somber period for San Diego. Growth was sluggish and there were setbacks. San Diego shrank when Coronado seceded in 1891. Two years later, Riverside County was carved from San Diego County, taking four million dollars of taxable property with it. There were bank failures: California National Bank went under in 1891 and in 1893, Consolidated National Bank and California Savings Bank followed. Even the aging Alonzo Horton felt the pinch of hard times as he was forced to sell off the plaza across the street from his hotel to the city for $10,000.

But hard times or not, San Diego hung on and occasionally even moved ahead a little. An experiment with San Francisco-style cable cars was begun in June, 1890. The cars rattled along between five and ten miles an hour, riding cables pulled by two massive wheels in a powerhouse at Fourth and Spruce. But the San Diego cable cars never caught on and, by March, 1892, the company was out of business. Tourmaline gems were discovered along the San Luis Rey River and in the foothills near Ramona and Julian. Within a few years, other gems, including topazes, were being mined.

A new lighthouse on the tip of Point Loma blinked on in 1891. The old lighthouse on the bluff above, though darkened, remained a favorite of tourists and picnicking locals. That same year, the San Diego Electric Railway was organized, binding the city with tracks. In 1898, during the Spanish-American War, an old iron gunboat, built just after the Civil War, wheezed into harbor. Her name was the U.S.S. *Pinta* and with her assignment to the port, the U.S. Navy became a permanent part of the San Diego scene.

The old Point Loma lighthouse, now part of Cabrillo National Monument, was not equipped with a foghorn. Keeper Robert Israel spent many a damp and lonely night on the beach, blasting away with his shotgun to warn off ships. Restoration of the "new" lighthouse was completed in March, 1984.

Lost Mysteries: In June, 1896, in Boston, an imperious, middle-aged woman named Katherine Tingley spoke to a gathering at the Tremont Theater. It was one of a series of speeches by "Madame Tingley," leader of the Universal Brotherhood and Theosophical Society, a splinter group from the Theosophical Society founded in 1875.

Madame Tingley promised that "when Theosophy has liberated all men ... the prisons will be emptied, wars will cease, hunger and famine will be unknown ... disease, which so often springs from evil acts and thoughts, will pass away ... and under the shadowing wings of the great brotherhood, all mankind will abide in peace, unity and love."

The following year found her in San Diego where her Brotherhood had purchased 130 acres of land on Point Loma. With appropriate rites, Madame Tingley laid the cornerstone for a "School for the Revival of the Lost Mysteries

---

Wobblies, Cultists, and those Flying Fools

Madame Tingley's "Lomaland," which faded out of existence in the 1930s, is recalled in the Greek Theater. It is a part of today's Point Loma College on Lomaland Drive.

of Antiquity." One by one, before the eyes of startled and amused San Diegans, strange and wonderful buildings began to rise on the Theosophical land. Among them was the first outdoor Greek Theater built in the United States, a gateway with Egyptian columns, and a temple crowned by glittering glass domes. A school was established where children studied Yoga and, wearing togas, performed Greek plays in the theater.

Many San Diegans were fascinated by the "Purple Mother of Lomaland" and her Theosophist followers. But some community religious leaders, certain that Theosophy was "opposed to the Gospel of Christ," grew suspicious and hostile. Both the Immigration Service and the State Board of Health took a hard look at Lomaland. The Los Angeles *Times* ran a lurid tale of a woman saved from forced labor at the hands of the bizarre cult. The feisty Mrs. Tingley promptly sued the *Times*, winning a judgment of $7500. Meanwhile, the Immigration Service and state health officials released reports completely clearing the Theosophists.

In February, 1898, a man with a more wordly outlook set up a strange-looking box on a downtown San Diego street. If the man had come only 30 years before, he would have seen a raw frontier town of adobe and wood. But San Diego had changed in both appearance and outlook. Peering into the box,

City of Dreams: Madame Tingley's Theosophical civilization on Point Loma was somewhat baffling, but benign.

A Short History of San Diego

he began turning a crank attached to its side. The man was from the Thomas Edison Company and he was making a movie. The silent, flickering result was only 25 feet long and showed a double-decked trolley rumbling past and a growing city of steel and stone. The Edison Company called the film "Street Scene, San Diego, California."

The cool, gray morning of January 1, 1900, came quietly to San Diego. A stroller along the waterfront, peering across the bay, could make out the gaily colored tents of "Tent City" at the Hotel Del Coronado, where families "roughed it in style." In snug homes with picket fences, people sipping their coffee and opening the morning *Union* wondered what the new century would bring.

The first years saw steps taken to make certain San Diego's natural beauty survived. In the sumer of 1902, a Park Improvement Committee was formed, and plans were made to transform 1,400 scrubby, rattlesnake-infested acres into the lush jewel that is today Balboa Park. The Committee's plans incorporated the work of nursery owner Kate Sessions, who had been quietly landscaping the park for a decade, planting 100 new trees a year.

By 1908, San Diego had sprawled far beyond Alonzo Horton's carefully laid-out streets. Over 40,000 people now called San Diego home. That year, city planner John Nolan made a careful study of San Diego. He was not impressed. In his *San Diego: A Comprehensive Plan for Its Improvement*, he wrote:

> Notwithstanding its advantages of situation, climate and scenery, San Diego is today neither interesting nor beautiful. The city is not thoughtful, but, on the contrary, ignorant and wasteful. It has no wide and impressive business streets, practically no open spaces in the heart of the city, no worthy sculpture. Aside from the big, undeveloped City Park, it has no pleasure grounds, parkways nor boulevards, no large, well-arranged playgrounds. It has no public buildings excellent in design and location. It has done little or nothing to secure for its people the benefits of any of its great natural resources, nor to provide those concomitants without which natural resources are so often valueless . . . Fortunately, the public-spirited men and women of San Diego are preparing to act in time.

Nolan's recommendations, which included improving the bay front and building a civic center, were noted, though not followed. But the seed of civic awareness had been planted and would grow. And Nolan would again be called upon by San Diego and asked for advice.

Warships and Planes: The new century also saw an increasing military impact in San Diego. Not far from Mrs. Tingley's shining glass domes, Fort Rosecrans stood watch over the harbor. On the dreary flats of North Island, Fort Pico was under construction. And more and more,

Within a few years of Edison's San Diego film, five major motion picture companies had studios here, including the Essanay Company, which produced the popular "Bronco Billy" westerns. But by 1913, they had all moved on—some to a farming area near Los Angeles called Hollywood.

Land for a huge city park had been set aside in 1868, but for decades no one knew quite what to do with it.

In 1900, in response to a long-running bicycle craze, San Diego posted its first speed limit: bicycle riders could not peddle faster than eight miles an hour.

the black smoke columns rising into San Diego's air came from the funnels of navy warships. The potential of the great bay had not escaped Washington.

Just how much the navy had become part of the city's life was shown in 1905 when the boilers on the gunboat *Bennington* exploded with a murderous roar, killing 60 men. San Diego mourned as though the dead sailors had been her sons. Hundreds streamed out to Point Loma, where the *Bennington* dead were buried in a mass grave and a monument was raised in their memory.

In 1908, the battleships of the "Great White Fleet," on their way around the world in a demonstration of America's growing naval power, anchored offshore. Jubilant San Diegans built bonfires on the beach in greeting and rowed out to the ships with boatloads of San Diego-grown oranges. Because of their size, the battleships had not been able to enter the harbor. But there was already talk in the War Department of dredging the bay so that the heavier, more powerful warships to come could use it.

Three years later, naval aviation was launched in San Diego Bay. On February 17, pioneer aviator Glenn Curtiss' float-equipped biplane landed on the bay, and gently taxied up to the heavy cruiser *Pennsylvania*, where a crane plucked the dripping plane from the water and deposited it on deck. The crane then returned it to the water. Curtiss' engine coughed into life and the plane lifted off and flew to North Island. It was obvious to the naval officers who watched the demonstration that airplanes could indeed serve as the eyes of a ship at sea. Impressed, the navy appropriated $25,000 to help develop the new field of naval aviation.

In 1912, the navy sent its first fledgling pilots to San Diego to train in three cloth and wood-framed airplanes at North Island. Calm mornings on the bay were soon assaulted by the sputter and pop of aircraft engines. It was less than a decade since the Wright Brothers had first wobbled into the air over the sands of Kitty Hawk.

Dictator: Southern California felt the repercussions of the Mexican revolt against Porfírio Díaz.

The revolt was bloody but not always epic; Mexicali was taken by eight men.

Red Flag Over Tijuana: In 1910, revolution exploded throughout Mexico as peasant armies rose against dictator Porfirio Díaz. At first, the dusty, ramshackle bordertowns of Baja California escaped the civil war. But in 1911 they fell one by one to rebel forces who invaded, not from the south, but from the United States. American neutrality had been violated and both Washington and Mexico City were enfuriated. U.S. Army units marched south from Fort Rosecrans to patrol the border as rebel flags flew in Mexicali and Tecate.

Mexico City was not sure quite what to make of the "rebel forces" along the border. Unlike the revolutionary armies of Emiliano Zapata and Pancho

A Short History of San Diego

Warships: In the early 1900s, navy vessels became common in the bay. That is indeed laundry hanging on the rigging of the USS Ranger.

Warplanes: Rockwell Field's aircraft and facilities were crude but rapidly improving in the century's first quarter.

Villa fighting in the Mexican interior, these rebels were a ragtag collection of drifters, opportunists, and idealists. Many of them came from the ranks of the socialist International Workers of the World, nicknamed the "Wobblies." In January, 1911, Jack London expressed the solidarity many radicals felt for the Revolution: "We socialists, anarchists, hoboes, chicken thieves, outlaws and undesirable citizens of the U.S. are with you heart and soul. You will notice that we are not respectable. Neither are you. No revolutionary can possibly be respectable in these days of the reign of property!"

For a while the Wobbly volunteers were led by a U.S. Marine deserter named Jack Mosby. But, in preparation for an attack on Tijuana, they held an election to select a new general. The winner was a Welsh adventurer named Caryl Pryce who had had experience fighting in the British army in India and South Africa.

On May 10, 1911, Pryce led his small army in a dawn attack on Tijuana. After a brief but vicious battle, the town was taken. Soon, curious San Diegans peering across the border with telescopes could make out a bright red flag fluttering over the town. On it were the words *Tierra y Libertad*—land and liberty.

I.W.W. leader Jack Mosby was arrested as a deserter from the Marines and was shot attempting to escape. Caryl Pryce eventually went to Hollywood to act in westerns.

Mexican government troops were soon on the march north from Ensenada, determined to retake Tijuana. With Mosby back in command (Pryce having decided the cause was already lost), the rebels moved south on June 22. Within three hours the battle was over, and the shattered rebel survivors fled across the border to internment at Fort Rosecrans.

Firehoses and Billy Clubs: The Wobblies were done with the Mexican Revolution, but they were far from finished with San Diego. I.W.W. members streamed into San Diego from all over the United States to agitate against capitalism. Many San Diegans loathed the I.W.W., calling them the "I Won't Works." Harsh words flew back and forth—the mood grew increasingly ugly.

For decades, "Join the I.W.W." and "Viva Villa!" could be seen in faded letters on a brick wall across from the Market Street Police Station. In the early 1980s, the wall with its defiant words was torn down.

Finally, on March 10, 1912, violence broke out as police found themselves facing an angry mob milling outside the city jail, where a number of Wobblies were being kept on charges of having broken a recently passed ordinance banning street corner speeches. The Fire Department was called in and high-pressure hoses turned on the mob. Meanwhile, vigilante groups started forming.

Several times in the following weeks, the I.W.W. attempted to reorganize in San Diego but without success. On April 12, the *Union* ran a proclamation of "The Vigilantes": "We propose to keep up the deportation of these undesirable citizens . . . as fast as we can catch them, and hereafter they will not only be

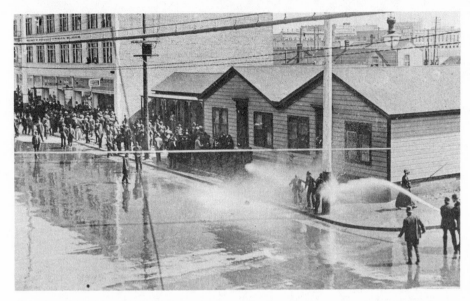

Riot: I.W.W. supporters find refuge from high pressure hoses as San Diego firemen and police clear the streets.

carried to the county line and dumped there, but we intend to leave our mark on them in the shape of tar rubbed into their hair, so that a shave will be necessary to remove it, and this is what these agitators (all of them) may expect from now on, that the outside world may know that they have been to San Diego."

Two months after the city jail riot, anarchist Emma Goldman (known to her admirers as "Splendid Emma") arrived in San Diego. But she was forced onto a train in the middle of night and sent on her way. The next morning, the *Union* reported that "Emma Goldman, anarchist leader and defender of the I.W.W. is speeding on her way to Los Angeles and her manager, Dr. Ben Reitman, is said to be somewhere on his way to Los Angeles, clad thinly in his underwear and a coat of tar and feathers acquired somewhere on the Penesquitas Ranch twenty miles to the north of this city after being forced to kneel and kiss the Stars and Stripes and promise solemnly never again to return to San Diego." Thus the "Socialist Revolution in San Diego" ended with Emma Goldman looking out of a train on her way out of town.

"In that town called San Diego when the workers try to talk,
The Cops will smash them with a sap and tell 'em 'take a walk,'
They throw them in a bull pen and they feed them rotten beans,
And they call that 'law and order' in that city, so it seems."

—I.W.W. Song

The Exposition: Not long afterward, as if to clear the air, something wonderful began to happen on the hills and canyons of Balboa Park. A city spun from dreams was beginning to rise, created out of concrete, wood, chicken wire, and plaster. Built to house the Panama-California

In its first year, the Panama-California Exposition had to compete with San Francisco's even more spectacular Panama-Pacific International Exposition. San Diego's celebration was assured a second year by timely loans from Los Angeles and local boosters.

Exposition, the dream city was intended to be more than a random collection of temporary exhibit halls. A small town was created that evoked the romantic atmosphere of Old Spain. San Diego later not only kept the permanent buildings but in many cases refused to tear down the temporary plaster ones, which are still a part of the park today, either lovingly preserved or carefully duplicated in concrete.

As the *Saturday Evening Post* said: "The buildings [in San Diego] are beautiful, the setting is lovely...the note of San Diego's fair is simply charm."

On January 1, 1915, the first crowds entered the Exposition over the graceful new bridge spanning Cabrillo Canyon. Future president Franklin D. Roosevelt visited the Exposition twice as Assistant Secretary of the Navy. The Vice President of the United States came and so did movie stars and two ex-presidents, Theodore Roosevelt and William Taft. And thousands of local families came carrying picnic baskets. Indians danced before a plaster-and-paint New Mexico pueblo and brass bands marched down the Prado. The Exposition ran for two happy, gaudy years.

The Big Wet: Even in the wettest winters, the rainfall in San Diego is not enough to meet the city's needs. A dry winter can spell disaster unless water is brought in from elsewhere. In 1916, San Diego had suffered through four years of drought, and the water level in the city reservoirs was dangerously low. In desperation, the city turned to a dapper little man with slicked-down hair named Charles Hatfield, who claimed to be a rainmaker. For $10,000, he promised to fill the Morena Reservoir to overflowing.

In early January, 1916, Hatfield and his brother Paul climbed a tall wooden platform near the reservoir. Once on top, they mixed mysterious chemicals which they refused to identify. Then, incredibly, the first rain drops fell into the dust at the base of the platform. A light rain started. Within minutes, the rain became heavy and the sky was filled with rolling black clouds. Four days and 13 inches later, it was still raining.

For a short time there was a break in the clouds and a soggy San Diego tried to dry out. But then it rained again. The placid San Diego River raged out of control. Mission Valley was soon a vast sheet of water as houses and barns disappeared. Bridges cracked and were swept away. Lower Otay Dam crumbled, and 13 billion gallons of water roared down the canyons and into the sea. In its wake it left a seven-mile strip of death and destruction as ranches and farms and orchards were destroyed.

In the aftermath, Charles Hatfield presented his bill to the city for $10,000.

Rainmaker: Charles Hatfield
mixes his secret ingredients.

The city agreed to pay if Hatfield would accept the millions of dollars in property damage suits that were piling up as a result of the flood. Hatfield bowed out and went to make rain elsewhere, certain his only fault was in doing too good a job.

Wouldn't it be Wonderful: The Panama-California Exposition was winding down in late 1916. That September, a local doctor and his brother were driving down Sixth Avenue past Balboa Park. As they passed the Exposition grounds, they were startled to hear a lion's distant roar. The lion was part of a small group of animals on display at the Exposition. The doctor turned to his brother.

"Wouldn't it be wonderful," said Doctor Harry Wegeforth, "to have a zoo in San Diego?"

The Splendid Obsession

10

At the entrance to the San Diego Zoo, there is a large bust of Dr. Harry Wegeforth. The expression on the face is kindly. But photographs of the man show a firm, set mouth and sharp eyes behind owlish glasses. Somewhere between the two images of gentleness and sternness is the real Harry Wegeforth.

Despite a quarter of a century in the public spotlight building and battling for his zoo, Wegeforth was a private man. It was not until after his death in 1941 that his personal record of the Zoo's early days was found. In 1953, these remembrances were published by the Zoological Society as *It Began With a Roar*. It's through this collection of Wegeforth's thoughts and memories that the Zoo's path can be traced from weekend project to splendid obsession. Starting with a random collection of animals in cramped cages, he laid the foundation for what is today one of the finest zoos in the world. His tenaciousness charmed some and angered others. He could be pugnacious in his pursuit of excellence. Millionaire John D. Spreckels once warned, "Watch out for this Wegeforth. If you're a patient, you get your tonsils or your appendix out. But if you're working on the zoo, you get cut off at the pockets!"

Naval Mascots: Wegeforth's passing remark to his brother, "Wouldn't it be splendid if San Diego had a zoo!" has become part of the city's folklore. Within a few days the dream was being transformed into reality. On September 27, 1916, a San Diego *Union* article told of the doctors Harry and Paul Wegeforth who "are interested in the promotion of a zoological society for San Diego." The article quoted Harry Wegeforth: "We already have a good start in the collection we have at the Exposition . . . There are tons of animals from Mexico, Central and South America coming through

Opposite page
**Founder: A beaming
Dr. Harry Wegeforth astride
a baby Indian elephant in
1923.**

our port and being distributed among cities like Chicago, New York and San Francicso. These animals are gifts. Why can't we keep some of them here?"

In early October, the Zoological Society of San Diego Board of Directors, five men including Harry and Paul Wegeforth, held its first meeting. The new society's constitution and by-laws were based on those of the New York Zoological Society.

The Zoo's operating costs for February, 1917, totaled $95.67. Today the Zoo is a $44 million-a-year corporation in which a single animal, like the Okapi, can be worth in excess of $100,000.

The Zoo's first animals were gleaned from leftover Panama-California Exposition exhibits throughout Balboa Park. The Board of Park Commissioners awarded the fledgling Zoological Society supervision over the animals, and the city council threw in a collection of peeling wood and wire cages that had lined Park Boulevard to temporarily house them.

A herd of elk were brought up from their corral south of the organ pavilion. A pair of bears was brought over from their exhibit on the west side of the park next to Sixth Avenue. A flock of ducks and a cage to hold them was donated by Joseph Sefton, Jr. A small herd of buffalo was led across the Laurel Street Bridge.

Well-meaning San Diegans began showing up with all sorts of local wild life from harbor seals to rattlesnakes. Another source of animals was a stream of naval mascots who had outlived their welcome. These included bears who had grown too large, monkeys that bit, and snakes who liked to curl up in warm places in ship's engines. Some of the donated animals were added to the Zoo's collection while others were sold or traded off.

It was always Wegeforth's intention that the Zoo be more than a passive collection of exhibits. Instead, it would reach out to its visitors, both entertaining and educating them. In early 1917, only a few months after the Zoo's founding, the Junior Zoological Society of San Diego came into being. Children could enroll as members for a 50-cent fee. About the same time, the Zoo's educational department began a modest series of free Saturday afternoon lectures.

100 **Bone Dry Acres:** As the Zoo's collection grew, it became obvious that the wretched little cages along Park Boulevard were no longer sufficient. Balboa Park offered the best location for a permanent home, but it was public land and the Zoo was a private organization. Finally a compromise was struck. The Zoo's animals and facilities became the property of the City of San Diego. However, it would be administered by the private Zoological Society of San Diego.

In late 1921, the city gave 100 acres of Balboa Park to the Zoo as a

A Short History of San Diego

Early days: These wolf and coyote cages on Park Boulevard were soon improved when the Zoo moved to new quarters in Balboa Park.

permanent home. Renowned today for its lush greenery, Balboa Park in the 1920s was still like a desert. And those 100 bone-dry, rattlesnake-infested acres were in the remote, northern part of the park.

On the site were four mesas surrounded by winding canyons. To the casual observer, the mesas, with their scrawny bushes and rutted soil, looked fit for only the horned toads that skittered across the rocks. But for the determined Harry Wegeforth, they were perfect.

As he later recalled in *It Began With a Roar*:

The Balboa Park of the 1920s was indeed rattlesnake infested. In 1922, two boys and a girl were struck.

> There was nothing haphazard about the development of the Zoo . . . We wanted individual areas for each group of animals. Knowing with what malevolent speed diseases can spread among animals, we wanted these areas some distance apart so that if an epidemic broke out among the animals, that area could be isolated and the Zoo would not have to be closed. The layout of the Zoo grounds lent itself ideally to this end.

It was decided that an admission charge of ten cents was needed to cover construction and maintenance costs, although Wegeforth insisted that children be admitted free. To enforce the fee (and protect the animals) the Zoo needed a fence. Wegeforth met with newspaper heiress Ellen Browning Scripps and she agreed to pay for the fence. For the next decade, until her death in 1932, Ellen Scripps was a financial pillar and faithful friend of the Zoo.

In 1922, construction on the Balboa Park site began. By 1923, the animals had been removed from the cramped Park Boulevard cages which had been their home for more than five years. Several of the larger animals were installed in open grottoes similar to those of Hamburg's Hagenbeck Zoo. The zoo that some San Diegans had unimaginatively called "Wegeforth's Folly," was now a permanent part of the city.

One unusual trade was a 1938 swap with a private New Hampshire zoo. In return for valuable snakes, the eastern zoo asked for several shipments of California's finest fleas for a "flea circus."

Snake Trappers: In the 1920s, the Zoo paid part of its expenses with a thriving business in local snakes. Regular Zoo expeditions ferreted out rattlesnakes still hiding in the nooks and crannies of Balboa Park, and there was a standing cash award to local snake trappers. In 1925, one San Diego teenager was paid $40 for 17 serpents which the Zoo resold or traded to other zoos.

The animal collection continued to grow, sometimes in unorthodox ways. When the Marines landed in Nicaragua in 1925, Wegeforth fired off a telegram offering "prize money" for any interesting specimens the men might encounter. Some animals came in trades with other zoos (thus avoiding the expensive and often brutal professional animal traders). One of the first traders was the Honolulu Zoo, which sent several antelopes and rare Hawaiian birds. In January, 1925, the *Union* reported "the arrival of what is believed to be the rarest collection of Australian animals ever exported." Included in the Australian collection were two koalas, the only ones outside Australia.

In January, 1925, the San Diego *Sun* announced that even more "weird animals [were] due." The paper reported that the Zoo already boasted "enough kangaroos to hold 'kangaroo court' every day in the month and enough weird birds and snakes to provide a Dantesque picture of Delirium Tremens."

The year 1926 proved to be especially eventful. In January the first issue of *Zoonooz Magazine* appeared. It had originally been a column in the *Sun*; as a magazine filled with chatty notes on animal arrivals and other zoo events, it was published bi-monthly at ten cents a copy. Over the years, it has evolved into an award-winning monthly magazine.

In June, the first tour bus wound its way down the Zoo's canyons. That same year, Wegeforth boarded the navy tug *Koka* for a 250-mile trip south to Guadalupe Island, where the Zoo's first Zoological Expedition captured four elephant seals.

Arabian Oryx: *Oryx leucoryx*, an endangered species.

Firing Frank Buck: Wegeforth was known as a man who would not tolerate the abuse of animals. Treating an animal badly could lead to a reprimand and even a firing, as Frank Buck of "Bring 'Em Back Alive" fame learned. Buck, a noted big game hunter, was hired in 1922 as zoo director. However, Wegeforth and others found that he treated the animals roughly. In September, 1923, Buck was abruptly dismissed. The following year he sued the Zoo for $22,500, claiming that he had given up his profitable animal-trading business for the Zoo only to have Wegeforth interfere with his work. Zoo officials responded by pointing out that Buck had often treated the animals harshly. At the conclusion of a long and angry hearing, Superior Court Judge Gordon Andrews ruled in favor of the Zoo. Buck returned to what the *Union* called a "more spectacular career as wild animal man."

The 1920s also saw a bitter quarrel erupt as San Diego's Park Commission sought to place the Zoo under city control. The matter was put to a public vote in 1925. Proposition Six, if passed, would have allowed the Zoological Society to continue administration of the Zoo. If it failed, the Zoo's management was to be put in the hands of the city.

White Rhinoceras: *Ceratotherium simum,* an endangered species.

Under the rallying cry of "Keep the Zoo out of politics!" Wegeforth and his supporters urged that the proposition be passed. The Park Commission countered by claiming that the proposition would place "control of a large portion of the Park, together with thousands of dollars of city property, out of the hands of the people and place it in the hands of a private organization [the Zoological Society] over which the people have no control whatsoever."

A battle of ads was waged in the newspapers. The "Balboa Park Preservation Committee and Staunch Friends of the Zoo," including such powers as department store magnate George Marston, former congressman William Kettner, and Planning Commission Chairman Julius Wangeheim, campaigned for city control.

Wegeforth led the pro-Proposition Six forces. One of his most controversial ads was the "Children's Vote Sample Ballot." For several days, a ballot was printed in the newspapers asking San Diego's children to either vote yes because "I want my zoo kept out of politics," or no, because, "I don't care what becomes of the elephants and ponies and other animals." The children were then instructed to bring the ballot to the Zoo where they would be treated to ice cream, cake, and a movie.

In the end, the proposition passed. The Zoo's management has remained in the hands of the Zoological Society since. But for some San Diegans, the bitterness of the hard fight remained for a long time afterward.

One and Only: In late 1931, while performing surgery, Wegeforth suffered a heart attack. While recovering, he realized that he had to cut back on his work load, so he gave up his medical practice in order to devote himself to the Zoo. But, as the Zoo continued to expand, he also realized he needed help in its day-to-day operation. He found that help in Belle Benchley.

Mrs. Benchley first arrived at the Zoo in the fall of 1925 as a temporary bookkeeper. She had no education in biology or zoology, but she did have a strong work ethic and a love for living things. She quickly acquired a practical

Mrs. Benchley: Here pictured in 1949 with baby gorillas Albert, Baba, and Bata.

education in the business of zookeeping. When the regular bookkeeper returned from vacation, Benchley was asked to stay on. Before long she had become Wegeforth's trusted assistant. In late 1926, she was appointed Executive Secretary of the Zoological Society, or Director of the Zoo.

In 1936, a writer for *Family Circle* magazine reported, ''Mrs. Benchley is a small, unassuming woman with soft hair and kind, friendly soft eyes. She wouldn't look out of place in a sunny kitchen with the smell of fresh baked bread around her. But, it seems, she's very much in place just where she is: Curator of the Zoo at Balboa Park in San Diego, California. Furthermore, she is unique, a 'one and only,' the one and only female curator of a zoo in the world.''

A Short History of San Diego

Jaguars from the Orinoco: By the mid-1930s, the San Diego Zoo was rapidly becoming world famous. Leaving the Zoo's daily operation to Belle Benchley, Wegeforth began searching the world for specimens. Sometimes he traveled on luxurious yachts, like Allan Hancock's sleek *Velero III* or Fred Lewis' *Stranger*. Other times, he sailed at his own expense on commercial steamers. His travels took him to remote spots, from the Amazon River and the Dutch East Indies to Australia and the South Pacific. Wherever he went he brought back new and exotic plants and animals for his beloved zoo: orangutans from Indonesia, turtles from the Philippines, and jaguars from the banks of the Orinoco River.

Throughout the Depression, the zoo, like the rest of the country, felt the pinch of hard times. But Wegeforth had long enjoyed a reputation as a first-rate scrounger. To keep the Zoo watered, for example, he had once clandestinely tapped into the city water lines. During the 1930s he showed that his determination was as firm as ever.

One of the most serious threats to the Zoo came in 1932 while Wegeforth was out of the country on an animal buying trip. San Diego County Assessor James Harvey Johnson decided that the Zoo owed $6358 in back taxes. Zoo officials and the City of San Diego replied that the Zoo was a nonprofit organization and should not be taxed. Assessor Johnson remained unmoved. When no tax money was forthcoming, he announced that the Zoo's animals would be auctioned off to pay the back taxes. In August, 1932, the auction was held despite the Zoo's protests.

But not a single bid was made. In desperation, Johnson declared the Zoo's animals to be the property of the State of California. Sacramento responded that, Johnson's zeal aside, the state did not own the Zoo. Furthermore, Sacramento was not at all certain that the auction had been legal. Besides, despite the Zoological Society's administration of the Zoo, the actual property and animals were city property and therefore non-taxable.

Two years later, in 1934, the Zoo's expenses were eased a little when voters agreed to a special tax of two cents on each $100 of assessed property value.

Despite the Depression, the Zoo continued to grow. By 1939, almost 2,000 new specimens been added.

Przewalski's horse: *Equus caballus przewalski,* discovered in Mongolia in the 1870s, it no longer exists in the wild.

Dogs and Cats: Back taxes were only one unusual threat to the Zoo. "Every once in a while," wrote Wegeforth in *It Began With a Roar*:

Balboa Park has an epidemic of some particular pest. First it was Airedale dogs. Many San Diegans had adopted these as pets, and suddenly the whole tribe was smitten with a desire to hunt through the park. They invaded Pepper Grove and killed five of the deer which were kept there. Later they chose the Zoo for their happy hunting ground. They would race outside the deer pens, barking so fiercely that several deer became panic-stricken and ran blindly into fences and trees and broke their necks. Then the Airedales took to climbing the seven-foot fences and attacking our kangaroos. Cats were our second plague . . . innumerable stray cats have raised good-sized families in the park. Anybody who had an unwanted old mother cat about to present the world with kittens would put her in the car and dump her in Balboa Park. There the cat had to fend for its own food and so preyed on the wild birds, as well as the food which we had provided for our Zoo animals. It seems strange that people who are so soft-hearted that they wouldn't send their cats to the Humane Society will abandon them to possible starvation.

Occasionally, zoo animals have dental problems. When Lucky the Elephant had a molar removed, it took a crow bar, electric drill, and sledgehammer.

By the end of the Depression, new fencing had largely taken care of the problem. Ironically, the same Depression that had seen private donations fall off brought help for the Zoo in the form of federal public service projects. Over two hundred additional employees were put to work on the Zoo grounds. With Works Progress Administration funds, the Zoo embarked on an ambitious construction program. By late 1936, bigger enclosures for the elephants and camels had been completed. Puddles the Hippo was moved into her new home with its large pond. An extensive sewer and water system was laid. A reptile house with Spanish tiles and arches was constructed. Nearby, a 1200-seat amphitheater was built and named Wegeforth Bowl. A 120-foot high flying cage was put up and filled with large birds of prey. And, noted a delighted Belle Benchley in the *Union*, "This gigantic undertaking, meant for the delight of men, women and children, cost the community not a cent. The entire program was a WPA project."

Okapi: *Okapia johnstoni,* **unknown to science before 1900.**

Work goes On: By 1941, Wegeforth's health had deteriorated badly. The previous year, while trading for animals in India, he had come down with both pneumonia and malaria. He was frail and tired easily. On June 24, 1941, he was taken by a friend, Joe Galven, to his tailor to be measured for two new suits. He never wore them; the next day Harry Wegeforth died. Many of the Zoo employees were dressed in their work clothes at his funeral. They had come directly from tending the Zoo's plants and animals. After the funeral, they returned to work.

For many San Diegans, Wegeforth personified the San Diego Zoo. Condolences from the rich and powerful and ordinary alike poured into both the Zoo and "Doctor Harry's" family. Two months after his death, a shipload of

A Short History of San Diego

Forcefeeding: Zoo visitors used to pay to help feed the likes of this woebegone python named Diablo.

animals, including three elephants, steamed into San Diego Bay from India. Harry Wegeforth's last animal shipment had arrived.

The War Years: Sunday afternoon, December 7, 1941, was clear and warm in San Diego. The Zoo was filled with visitors. Suddenly, over the loudspeakers, came orders for all servicemen to leave the Zoo at once and report for duty. Thus, for a number of San Diegans, World War II began.

The Zoo mobilized for war. Victory gardens were planted throughout the grounds. With gas strictly rationed, tour buses were put away for the duration. In the first year after Pearl Harbor, employees feared bombing; keepers were equipped with weapons in case dangerous animals escaped, and shutters were placed over the reptile house windows to prevent the escape of poisonous snakes.

With the exception of the Zoo and nearby golf course, Balboa Park was declared off-limits to civilians, and the park's museums were converted into hospitals. Zoo attendance soared as servicemen and war workers came to relax amid the animals and lush greenery. Wegeforth Bowl added an elephant show to its daily bear and seal shows.

The post-War years were quiet for the Zoo. The animal collection con-

Exotic birds arrived at the Zoo from Pacific battle-grounds throughout the war. One of the rarest, a Kagu bird, had been a gift to Admiral William F. Halsey from the government of New Caledonia.

tinued to grow steadily. In 1947, four Northern Fur Seals, the only ones in captivity, arrived. The Zoo's collections provided animals for European zoos that had been ravaged by the war. The London Zoo, for example, had been forced to kill its poisonous snakes to prevent their escape during the Battle of Britain. San Diego sent replacements, including rattlesnakes from the back country.

In 1953, Belle Benchley retired. She was presented with a trip around the world at her retirement party. True to form, she insisted on seeing the zoo in almost every foreign city she visited. Her legacy includes three books: *My Life in a Man-Made Jungle*, *My Friends the Apes*, and *My Animal Babies*.

Wgasa: In 1961, Zoo officials mapped out 1800 sun-browned acres near Escondido, approximately 50 miles from the Zoo. It was their dream that the empty hills and valleys would one day become a preserve for endangered plants and animals. At first, it was simply called the "Back Country Zoo." But by the late 1960s it was officially known as the Wild

Bushline: The Wgasa monorail passes by zebras, giraffes, and ostriches.

A Short History of San Diego

Symbol: The Zoo owes its famous koalas to the fact that they eat eucalyptus, a tree that thrives only in California and Australia. How they digest the highly acidic leaves is a mystery.

Animal Park. By 1970, it had been fenced in and the first breeding stock, cheetahs, had been introduced. Soon after, 20 rare white rhinos from South Africa were released into the Park. White rhinos had never reproduced well in captivity, but within a decade, 42 had been born in the Park.

The Wild Animal Park was opened to the public in May, 1972. It is as different from the traditional zoo of today as the San Diego Zoo was from the typical zoo of the 1920s. Rather than touring a series of animal enclosures, the visitor boards a monorail, the "Wgasa Bushline." As the Bushline moves slowly along the edge of the hills, the animals are seen much as if they were in the wild. It is an ever-changing show. There are warm afternoons when the animals drowse under the sun, and herds of antelope and zebra move across the veldt in a cloud of dust. In the evenings, the pride of lions stirs awake in the grass.

Less than a thousand acres of the Wild Animal Park have been developed so far, including the preserves and Nairobi Village with its exhibits and shops. Some of the rarest creatures on earth have found refuge amid its hills and canyons and waterholes. Several, like Przewalski's wild horses (only 300 remain) or the okapi (just 55 exist in all the world's zoos), have successfully reproduced. Each baby represents a step back from the edge of extinction.

Adult male African elephants are driven from matriarchal herds to wander as bad-tempered loners. Unlike most zoos, the Wild Animal Park has room for the elephants to breed and then be separated.

Cascade Canyon: Visitors look down on the Sitatunga's naturalized environment (see photo opposite).

Wegeforth's Legacy: An ambitious future is being planned for the San Diego Zoo. Exhibits established by Wegeforth over a half century ago are being replaced as they deteriorate with age. In 1982, the Whittier Southeast Asian Exhibit, the Zoo's first major renovation in over a decade, was dedicated. In 1984 came the Zoo-proclaimed ''Year of the Cat,'' with the redesigning of the big cat enclosures.

For several years prior to 1984, the Zoo had been engaged in an exchange of animals with zoos in the People's Republic of China. Among the animals sent to China have been emus, orangutans, rhinos, hippos, spider monkeys, and a variety of parrots and serpents. In return, San Diego has received 24 species of birds, reptiles, and mammals, seven of which are not seen anywhere else in the United States. In mid-1984, the San Diego Zoo became sister zoo to the Chengdu Zoo, in Sichuan Province. That November the Chengdu Zoo loaned San Diego two rare golden monkeys. The last golden monkey seen in the western world lived for two weeks in the London Zoo in 1939.

Iragelephus speki: **A rare aquatic antelope.**

In October, 1984, officials announced that the Zoo would be totally redesigned over the next three decades. Replacing the traditional zoo exhibit, where animals are grouped according to type, the new exhibits will feature a number of species in their natural, shared environments. The Zoo's education programs now reach over 100,000 students each year from preschool through college. Zoo visitors see animals rarely seen elsewhere, from koalas to graceful Mhorr gazelles, of which there are less than 100 in the world. At the Zoo's Center for Reproduction of Endangered Species, research continues on the survival of endangered species from pygmy chimps to snow leopards.

The Zoo is perhaps best known for its conservation work. Endangered animals have not only reproduced in Zoo refuges but, in some cases, have been reintroduced into the wild. In the early 1960s, only 100 graceful Arabian oryx survived. By 1981, the number had risen to 400 carefully protected individuals. Twenty oryx born in the Wild Animal Park were recently sent to preserves in the Middle East. Scientists at the Wild Animal Park are working for the day when a California condor, hatched in a Zoo nursery, will spread its wings and sail into the California sky.

This is Harry Wegeforth's legacy.

Five-Cent Apples and the Lone Eagle

11

Two forces crucial to San Diego's destiny began to appear in the early 1920s. The first was a growing military presence that, with its depression-proof payroll, would be an economic savior in hard times. In 1922, the San Diego Naval Training Station began training its first "boots," joining the nearby Marine Base, which had been commissioned in 1919. Also in 1922, a naval hospital was dedicated on a Balboa Park hillside overlooking the city. The following year saw the establishment of San Diego as headquarters of the Eleventh Naval District and the Pacific Fleet. The gray hulls of the navy ships became a familiar sight on San Diego Bay.

The second force that was to leave a keen mark on San Diego was the aviation industry, in 1920 still young and primitive. The city saw several aviation firsts. In 1922, Lt. Jimmy Doolittle flew from Jacksonville, Florida, to San Diego, in a record 21 hours. In 1923, the first photographs of a solar eclipse were taken above San Diego's clouds. That same year, the first airborne refueling was performed over the city. In 1925, using government-surplus biplanes, ex-army pilot T. Claude Ryan began ferrying passengers between San Diego and Los Angeles. Advertising as "Ryan Airlines," he offered the first flights by a regularly scheduled airline in the United States.

The early canvas tents and dusty landing fields on North Island disappeared. In their place were concrete landing strips, hangars, sea plane ramps, and repair shops. One of the few reminders of the "old" North Island were its jackrabbits. In the early 1920s, the military, which considered the rabbits a menace, declared war on them. Regular "rabbit roundups" were soon underway and hundreds of them were clubbed to death or driven into the bay. Sunday afternoons echoed to gunfire as hunters stalked those rodents that had escaped. Finally, in the late thirties, victory was declared and the hunts ceased.

Ryan Airlines never really caught on. Ryan soon returned to the more profitable businesses of flying the mail and building airplanes.

Opposite page
America's Hero: A boyish-looking Charles Lindbergh poses in San Diego shortly before his sensational flight.

Prince of Wales: The history of Edward VIII's abdication dates from this Del Coronado banquet in 1920.

The Prince: Throughout the Roaring Twenties, life remained pleasantly calm in San Diego. It was true that a railroad, financed by millionaire John D. Spreckels, now linked the city with the East. The San Diego and Arizona Railway wound through San Diego's eastern mountains and dipped into Mexico on its tortuous way to Yuma. For decades, long freight trains filled with San Diego's agricultural products rumbled east. But for the average San Diegan, Mr. Spreckels' railroad made little difference. Increasingly it was San Diego's rival, Los Angeles, that drew the nation's attention. In the early 1920s, that city showed a population of 576,000, more than San Francisco's 506,000 and far beyond San Diego's 74,000 residents.

In April, 1920, a handsome twenty-six-year-old man arrived in San Diego for a two-day visit that left the city agog with excitement. He was Edward Windsor, Prince of Wales, heir to the throne of England. On the evening of April 7, a ball was held at the Hotel Del Coronado in the Prince's honor. During the course of the evening, he briefly met Mrs. Earl Spencer, the wife of an American naval officer stationed in Coronado.

Several years later they met again in Leicestershire, England. She had divorced, remarried, and divorced again. The Prince fell deeply in love with the lady, now known as Mrs. Simpson. Barred from marrying her because of her divorces, Edward, now King of England, abdicated in 1936 rather than loose her. Soon after, he married Mrs. Simpson. And so it was that a former Coronado housewife became the Duchess of Windsor.

The 1920s saw communities wooing new residents with alluring names. National City was touted as being "Where Rail and Water Meet," while La Mesa called itself "The City of Beautiful Homes." Less charmingly, Ramona boasted of being "The Turkey Capital."

A 75% Chance: About two o'clock one lazy afternoon in February, 1927, while relaxing on his office porch, T. Claude Ryan received a telegram. It read, "CAN YOU CONSTRUCT WHIRLWIND ENGINE PLANE CAPABLE FLYING NONSTOP BETWEEN NEW YORK AND PARIS STOP IF SO PLEASE STATE COST AND DELIVERY DATE." It was signed "Robertson Aircraft Corporation" in St. Louis, but had in fact been sent by a tall, quiet former air mail pilot whose friends called him "Slim." His name was Charles Lindbergh.

A few days later, Lindbergh arrived in San Diego to meet with Ryan. After careful consultation, he signed a contract with Ryan for a modified M-1 monoplane that would serve one purpose: a solo flight across the Atlantic Ocean. Over lunch one afternoon, Ryan asked Lindbergh what he thought the chances were of a successful flight. Later, Ryan recalled, "He turned the question right back at me and said, 'What percentage would you say?'

"I really thought, because of the ever-present chance of failure of that single engine, and the weather risk, that it was only a little better than 50 percent, but to be more optimistic for his sake, I shot back my answer, 'I think you have about a 75 percent chance.' This courageous young man then said, 'That is about what I think, too.'"

Ryan and his workers, caught up in the fever of the coming flight, worked long hours on the *Spirit of St. Louis*. In *We*, Lindbergh's account of his famous flight, he wrote, "The personnel of the Ryan Airlines at once caught the spirit of the undertaking, and during the two months of constuction the organization labored as it never had before. Day and night, seven days a week, the structure grew from a a few lengths of steel tubing to one of the most efficient planes that has ever taken the air. During this time it was not unusual for the men to work twenty-four hours without rest, and on one occasion Donald Hall, the Chief Engineer, was over his drafting table for thirty-six hours."

On April 28, 1927, the sleek silver airplane was hitched to the back of Ryan's Studebaker and towed to desolate Dutch Flats. There, near where the main San Diego post office now stands, it lumbered down the flats on its first test flight. Within six seconds, the *Spirit of St. Louis* lifted into the air.

Twenty-two days later, Lindbergh headed for New York. On May 20, he took off from New York for a 33½ hour flight to Paris and into history.

In August, 1928, San Diego's new airport was dedicated. A mass flight of 222 military planes thundered overhead in salute. And soon after, the first commercial and private planes began flying into Lindbergh Field.

Since Lindbergh's funding for the expedition came from a group of St. Louis businessmen, the plane was named *The Spirit of St. Louis*.

Today, the only visible reminder of Lindbergh's Dutch Flats test flight area is a bronze tablet set in the wall of San Diego's Midway Drive Post Office.

Pioneer: Glenn H. Curtiss' Coronado flying school trained the first naval aviators.

Depression: San Diego youths demonstrate for the New Deal flanked by palms and eucalyptus.

Roosevelt's Alphabet Soup: San Diego's placid climate combined with its reliable military payroll to soften some of the hard edges of the Depression. As in other cities, there was the sad list of failed businesses, lost homes, and broken dreams. Soup kitchens opened and once-prosperous businessmen sold 5 cent apples on street corners. In 1933, a Communist demonstration flared into a riot that saw 30 demonstrators hurt and eight jailed. But as the *Union* pointed out in 1931, the Depression's "effects here are nothing like as severe as those reported from industrial and agricultural centers in other parts of the country."

The Depression bleakness was also brightened somewhat by President Franklin Roosevelt's "alphabet soup" of relief programs. The W.P.A. built zoo cages in Balboa Park, fair grounds and a race track at Del Mar, and a state college campus in east San Diego. Young men of the C.C.C. were hard at work clearing dead timber, hacking out trails, and planting trees in the Cuyamaca and Laguna Mountains. In 1931, the army patched up the crumbling old Point

Loma lighthouse. Two years later, the lighthouse was turned over to the National Park Service to be restored as the Cabrillo National Monument. Reuben Fleet's Consolidated Aircraft moved its factory from chilly Buffalo, New York, to San Diego in the same year, giving a much-needed shot in the arm to the city's economy.

Perhaps the worst of the Depression was reflected in the newly homeless gathered in migrant camps. Mostly dust bowl refugees, the migrants lived on the fringes of cities near fields where there was the possibility of work, however ill-paid. San Diego had its share of such miserable "Hoovervilles." One was thrown up on the sand south of Imperial Beach, another clung to the banks of the San Diego River in Mission Valley. The migrants existed on "Hoover Hogs" (jackrabbits) and bitterly displayed empty pockets turned inside out as "Hoover Flags."

The Depression would prove grimly resiliant, but by 1934, conditions in San Diego had begun to improve. Building permits increased, agricultural and fishing revenues were up, even tourism was on the rise. The city was cautiously optimistic. And in that optimism, San Diego decided to put on another fair.

In the 1930s, San Diego's city government was riddled with corruption. Police chiefs arrived and departed at the rate of almost one a year. The mayor was arrested for a hit and run accident and drunk driving—both in the city limousine.

No work, no eat: Hard times and hard words greeted dust bowl refugees in California's fertile valleys.

Five-cent Apples and the Lone Eagle

The Splendid Splinter: A San Diego native, Ted Williams starred for the hometown Clippers before moving up to Boston in 1939. He was baseball's greatest student of hitting.

A Short History of San Diego

High Purpose: As Los Angeles was to later use its 1932 Olympic Coliseum for the 1984 Games, San Diego decided to reuse many of the buildings from its rousingly successful 1915-16 Exposition. New buildings were added to those undergoing renovation. Some of the most intriguing of the new buildings have not survived. Gone, for example, are "Gold Gulch" (a miniature gold mining town), the Standard Oil "Tower to the Sun," and the Firestone Singing Fountains, which have been replaced by a parking lot in front of the municipal gymnasium (built as the "Palace of Varied Industries"). But other buildings remain. Today the Ford Music Bowl resounds to the music of the Starlight Opera. The nearby Ford Building, crowning a hill overlooking San Diego, is the home of the Aerospace Museum.

The California-Pacific Exposition opened on May 29, 1935 with high purpose. It promised to portray "dramatically the achievement of man in the West from the time Juan Rodriguez Cabrillo sailed into San Diego Bay and claimed Southern California for Spain, through the present and giving a glimpse of what the future promises."

As they had in 1915-16, the crowds came again to gawk, to laugh, and to be amazed. Wide-eyed little boys lined up on the midway to see the lurid "Crime Doesn't Pay" exhibit. Sally Rand danced with her fans, and "Alpha the Robot" cavorted on the Prado. Something new called "television" was demonstrated. The Exposition ran for two wonderful years, and for a while the Depression seemed a little lighter. For many, though, the hard times would continue for several more years.

Sunday, December 7, 1941, was mild as winter days in San Diego usually are. It was close to noon when the first bulletins came over the radio. Some San Diegans weren't even sure where Pearl Harbor was. But by evening, everyone knew. And no one would ever forget. At North Island, navy ships were already preparing for sea. Even as Pearl Harbor burned, San Diego was going to war.

Two of the more bizarre exhibits of the 1935 Exposition were "Midget Village," populated by midgets and dwarfs, and Zoro Gardens Nudist Colony, where spectators in bleachers watched nudists disport themselves, at least until the colony was shut down.

Pearl Harbor was home port for the Navy's battleships, but San Diego was port to the fleet's aircraft carriers. Six carriers, all safe from the havoc of December 7, 1941, were based at North Island.

Open All Night

12

Every American city was affected by World War II, but San Diego was transformed. Its quiet streets suddenly throbbed with life. Aircraft factories rang with the sound of work around the clock, and along Broadway, some cafes never closed. Long troop trains rolled in and out of the Santa Fe Depot. Darkened warships slipped out of the harbor and armed men patrolled the city's beaches.

The Japanese attack on Pearl Harbor burned itself into the American consciousness. Blinded by fury and frustration, the United States government lashed out at the Japanese-Americans who lived on the west coast. In the Congressional Record for December 15, 1941, Congressman John Rankin thundered, "I'm for catching every Japanese in America, Alaska and Hawaii now and putting them in concentration camps . . . Damn them! Let's get rid of them now!"

On February 19, 1942, President Franklin Roosevelt signed Executive Order 9066 allowing the War Department to round up and detain Japanese-Americans. By the end of the war, over 120,000 had been removed to desolate barbed-wire camps in places like Manzanar, California, and Poston, Arizona. Eighty percent came from California. Almost 2000 came from San Diego.

On December 15, 1941, Secretary of the Navy Frank Knox told newspaper reporters, "The most effective fifth column work of the entire war was done in Hawaii, with the possible exception of Norway." But it was a statement without basis in fact. Hawaii's large Japanese-American population remained steadfastly loyal, as did California's. There was no treachery. But the voices of Knox and others had been heard across America and even in Mexico, which was eager to prove its support for the American war effort. Within the first months of the war, Mexico rounded up most of the Japanese-Mexicans living near its west coast and shipped them inland.

With the war, the military took over large sections of San Diego County. On Rancho Santa Margarita near Oceanside, the Marines established Camp Pendleton. In El Cajon, they laid out Gillespie Field and trained parachutists. The Army camped on Torrey Pines Mesa and the Navy moved into Balboa Park.

Opposite page
Internment: California's Japanese, citizens or not, were among the first victims of World War II.

Casualty: The U.S.S. *California* was one of the eight battleships destroyed or damaged at Pearl Harbor.

On the Cabrillo National Monument's Bayside Trail, concrete housing and steel tracks are still visible. The Army maintained a large searchlight there to sweep the harbor's entrance.

Barrage Balloons: San Diego quickly settled down to the business of being at war. The population swelled with war workers and service people. To handle the sudden influx, the city streetcar company scrounged second-hand rolling stock from as far away as New York. Sand-bagged machine gun emplacements sprouted along isolated beaches to hold back enemy troops. Barrage balloons dangled over the city to snatch Japanese airplanes from the air. Cavalry patrols rode around reservoirs, watching for saboteurs. On Point Loma, the Cabrillo National Monument lighthouse was closed to visitors and painted in camouflage. Incoming ships were challenged in code from the lighthouse. If the proper signal was returned, submarine nets protecting the bay were opened, allowing the ship to pass.

As the war ground on, San Diego became a vast network of war industries, navy yards, training camps, air fields, and hospitals. On Kearny Mesa, an instant city suddenly appeared as the government assembled blocks of cookie-cutter houses for workers. Furniture stores ran ads offering ready credit for defense workers. San Diego Gas and Electric's "Reddy Kilowatt" logo was drawn with helmet and rifle as he guarded a large "V for Victory."

The city also offered entertainment for a war-weary people. Downtown movie theaters ran midnight "swing-shift matinees." Ballrooms like the

A Short History of San Diego

Crystal Pier in Pacific Beach, the Silverado in East San Diego, and the Pacific Square Ballroom downtown offered big band music. For a little over a dollar, San Diegans could dance to the music of Benny Goodman, Glen Miller, Les Brown, and Stan Kenton. But reminders of the war were never far away. One tourist guide, in recommending the San Diego Zoo, noted, "The names in the news of the South Pacific war area are to be seen on many zoo cages, giving the men in the service a chance to know something about the wild inhabitants of the lands they will one day free from Nipponese possession."

As the returning wounded increased, Balboa Park became a vast military hospital. By the end of the war, the Zoo was one of the few areas still open to civilians.

The Aquatic Center: In the war's closing months, some San Diegans were busily preparing for peace. They realized that, with the wartime factories silent, new jobs would be needed. They also knew that San Diego was not the same drowsy city it had been. The city had come to life, and it would not go back to sleep. The years of fear and rationing were over, and Americans felt a hunger to enjoy life.

Tourism seemed an attractive proposition. There were people across the country who had not enjoyed a vacation in years. With some work, San Diego could be made into a tourist mecca. Tourism was a clean industry, it would attract outside capital, and it would provide many service jobs. As long ago as 1919, the San Diego-California Club had promoted the city by taking out ads in eastern magazines. San Diego soon became synonymous with palm trees, a romantic Spanish heritage, and pretty girls on sun-kissed beaches.

For years there had been talk of turning the mudflats of Mission Bay into a recreational center. In April, 1945, San Diego voters approved a two million dollar bond that allowed for the first dredging and roads. "Mission Bay," announced a 1945 citizen's committee press release, "with virtually unlimited opportunities for recreation, will make San Diego the aquatic center of the west coast, and give us a tourist attraction that will lure thousands of pleasure seekers annually." Mission Bay was built, but other grand projects weren't. Among the abandoned schemes were a civic ice skating rink, a Farmer's Market in Point Loma, and various additions to Balboa Park.

San Diego's population doubled to almost 400,000 during World War II. Many who had first arrived as war workers remained; more than one newlywed couple set up housekeeping in a war surplus tent.

As much as $18,000: The two forces that shaped San Diego's future in the 1950s were its exploding population and a growing dependence on the automobile. San Diego did not escape the post-war housing crunch. In 1946, Arizona investor Fred Winship brought three square blocks of prime La Jolla real estate. Soon he was offering lots at $12,000 to $25,000.

Within a few years, inexpensive La Jolla land was a nostalgic memory. In other parts of the city, the story was the same. By 1954, houses that had sold for as little as $5,000 in 1940 had shot up to $18,000. And new houses commanded even higher prices.

By the 1960s, the number of two-year community colleges in San Diego had swelled from one to seven.

More people meant more cars. By 1948, the lily pads under Balboa Park's Cabrillo Bridge had disappeared, replaced by a highway. In early 1951, there were already four major freeway interchanges. Freeways led to suburban growth and those suburbs were served by the massive new shopping centers.

The Jets Arrive: Aviation, a part of San Diego's heritage since Curtiss' flying school on North Island, continued to play a leading role in San Diego's affairs. Starting in the late 1940s, San Diego's windows rattled to the shriek of jets. In April, 1945, an early jet squealed onto the deck of an aircraft carrier in the bay, making the first jet-propelled landing. In September of that year, Lindbergh Field proudly opened a new runway, the largest in the west. Mid-1947 saw the first twin-engine pressurized airplane take off from San Diego. Seven years later, a helicopter lifted off from its San Diego base on the first non-stop transcontinental helicopter flight.

But the aviation industry also proved to be fickle. In 1959, Convair, dealt a severe blow by the failure of its 880 and 990 jet transport programs, began laying off the first of an eventual 21,000 workers. The new trend was toward missiles. Local aircraft companies began considering new products, from rockets to high-technology mass-transit sytems.

Roar of Jackhammers: The reshaping of the community's face to meet new needs is a San Diego tradition dating from the first settlers. The padres moved the mission from hillside to river bank. The soldiers of the Presidio came down from the hill to build Old Town. A century later, the citizens of Old Town moved next to the bay to build New Town. The 1960s saw San Diego's man-made geography change again.

Downtown San Diego's skyline, which had remained static for decades, was being altered. Layer by layer, skyscrapers climbed while some landmarks were broken into pieces to be carted away. For years, the uniformity of the downtown cityscape had been pierced only by the El Cortez Hotel, standing in solitary splendor on its hill. In 1963, the first of the new highrises, the 20-story Home Federal Building, opened its doors for business. Within four years,

Marilyn: Taking a break from *Some Like It Hot,* Marilyn Monroe poses with husband Arthur Miller and director Billy Wilder in 1959. The Hotel Del Coronado played a 1920s Florida resort in the film.

another 12 skyscrapers were up. Throughout the 1960s, the downtown streets echoed to the roar of jackhammers and the grinding of cranes.

In the heart of downtown, a cluster of striking new government buildings, the Community Concourse, was taking form. Construction did not begin without controversy. Voters had turned down five successive referendums to fund the concourse, which included a convention center. But city officials borrowed money from the city employees retirement fund and went ahead. In 1963, ground was broken. Two years later, the Community Concourse, with convention center, city hall, parking structure, and the elegant Civic Theater, was dedicated.

Turbulent Years: In the late 1960s, the social unrest spreading across America arrived in conservative San Diego. Segregation, for example, though not sanctioned by law, hemmed minorities in by social and economic prejudice. Of San Diego's 115 elementary schools in 1965, 41 had no black students whatsoever. Yet Stockton Elementary School in the over-crowded heart of southeast San Diego had a student body that was over 91 percent black. San Diego's de facto ghettos never exploded into mob violence as did Watts in 1965; but the long hot summer nights of the late 1960s still echoed to the sound of police, fire, and ambulance sirens.

The University of California at San Diego registered its first students in 1960. One student complained that the neighborhood, plush La Jolla, was "upper rent, upper class and upper tight."

Water World: Dredged from mud flats after World War II, Mission Bay Park is 4,600 acres of aquatic sports and activities, from water skiing to picnics on the beach.

The 1960s also saw a growing pride in their heritage by San Diego's Chicano citizens. Hispanics are a vital part of every San Diego community, and in some communities, such as Barrio Logan or San Ysidro, they are the majority. Still, despite their population and economic impact, the Mexican-Americans were often neglected by the city's business and civic leaders. But barrio residents like José Gomez and Rachel Ortiz began to be heard in city hall. On college campuses, MECHA, a Chicano student organization, came into being. A Balboa Park water tank, cleaned and covered with colorful murals, was converted into a Chicano Cultural Center. Plans for a California Highway Patrol headquarters in the shadows of the Coronado Bridge were shelved as residents successfully fought for a community park. Today, in place of the proposed CHP parking lot, are the green lawns of Chicano Park. The concrete bridge columns marching across the park have been converted by Chicano artists, like Salvador Torres, into bold statements of Hispanic pride.

San Diego had its share of student and counter-culture protests during the tumultuous 1960s and early 1970s. But most of the native hippies and New Left firebrands sought refuge in San Francisco and Berkeley, for San Diego was and is in many ways a conservative city. And it's a Navy town, with all the institutionalized patriotism that implies; in 1967, a study found that 25 percent of the city's 672,000 inhabitants were in some way connected with the navy either as personnel, dependents, employees, or contractors.

The tragic war in Vietnam left its mark on San Diego in a number of ways. Perhaps the most lasting is the tens of thousands of Vietnamese refugees who arrived here after the fall of Saigon in 1975. In the summer of that year, 20,000 immigrants were encamped at Camp Pendleton. Many of the newcomers have dispersed, but San Diego's Indochinese population, struggling heartily to make its way in America, numbers between eight and ten thousand. University Avenue between 33rd and 54th Streets has become a center for this newest wave in a nation of immigrants.

Into the 80s

13

During the boom of the 1880s, downtown San Diego was vibrantly alive. Large, ornate buildings lined the streets as testaments of faith in the city's future. A century later, the downtown has become the site of an urban renaissance as San Diegans again demonstrate that faith. In September, 1984, the San Diego *Daily Transcript*'s annual Downtown Capital Survey noted, "$2.4 billion of new construction has been recently completed, is under way or planned in downtown San Diego." As recently as two decades before, a future investment of such magnitude would have been regarded as unbelievable.

Like many American cities, post-World War II San Diego had suffered from a slow inner-city decay. Retail business moved to the suburban shopping malls. The San Diego *Union* and *Tribune* moved their presses to Mission Valley. The movie theaters that during the war had offered "midnight matinees" followed the suburban exodus or shifted to "adult" or third-run films. The building of the Community Concourse in the mid-1960s was a milestone in the revitalization of the city's downtown. It was one of the first hints that San Diego, like many major American cities, was ready to experience what Dr. Dipak Gupta of San Diego State University has called a "historic . . . third phase in the configuration of cities . . . a return to the city to live."

The 1980s will be remembered as the decade of San Diego's downtown revitalization. New towers like the Wells Fargo Building on Broadway and the Hotel Intercontinental just south of Seaport Village already dominate the skyline. Even more ambitious plans are in the offing. One of the more spectacular projects is the $800 million, 17-acre Santa Fe Development. Set along Pacific Highway near the Santa Fe Depot, the project calls for a vast complex of shops, restaurants, offices, and a major hotel. Included are five high-rise buildings.

Opposite page
Pleasure Fleet: Almost lost in a forest of masts, the San Diego Yacht Club on Shelter Island reigns over a private navy of thousands of cruisers and sailboats. The skyscrapers of the city's booming downtown rise across the Bay.

The centerpiece of the downtown renaissance is the Horton Plaza development: more than six blocks of theaters, cafes, a farmers' bazaar, deluxe hotel, specialty shops, and four major department stores. Across Broadway from the Plaza, the venerable U.S. Grant Hotel has been refurbished in an $80 million renovation project. Between the U.S. Grant and the Horton Plaza retail complex is Horton Plaza itself, restored to its turn-of-the-century elegance.

"Downtown San Diego's redevelopment," noted the Centre City Development Corporation's Kathy Kalland, "is changing not only the city's skyline but also its character and heartbeat. People who live, work or play downtown gladly overlook the temporary inconveniences of construction barricades, rerouted streets and swirling dust in expectation of the future."

The Gaslamp Quarter: One of the first areas to stir was also one of San Diego's most blighted: the Gaslamp Quarter, running south along Fifth Avenue. Once the heart of the 1880s boom, the quarter had deteriorated into some of the toughest blocks in San Diego. Street after street was lined with porno shops, greasy spoon cafes, cheap bars, and flop house hotels. Old line firms that had been there for decades, like San Diego Hardware (1892) and Ferris and Ferris Drugs (1887) carried on as best they could.

But in the 1970s, private firms and individuals began moving into what *San Diego Magazine* called "The Urban Frontier." The architectural firm of Macy, Henderson and Cole restored the 1882 Yuma Building. Shirley Bernard took over and cleaned up the 1887 Grand Pacific Hotel. Eugene and Marilyn Marx restored the 1906 Hotel Lester. In 1974, the Gaslamp Quarter Association (now the Gaslamp Quarter Council) was founded as more businesses moved into the area and upgrading continued. Today, the Council is administered by an elected 21-member board of directors. Each director either has an investment in or is a resident of the Gaslamp Quarter.

Brick sidewalks were laid and turn-of-the-century streetlamps installed. More buildings, like the 1890 Keating Building and the ornate 1888 Louis Bank of Commerce, were restored. Some, like the 1910 Knights of Pythias Building, were demolished to make way for new construction. On F Street, the 1887 Horton-Grand, with its graceful iron grillwork, was carefully taken apart by developer Dan Pearson and, combined with the Victorian Kahle Saddlery/Brooklyn Hotel building, completely restored as a Gaslamp bed and breakfast inn. Pearson's future plans include restoring the Grand Pacific Hotel (which he now also owns) to its former glory.

Home port to 118 ships and 118,000 uniformed personnel, San Diego is the largest navy complex in the world.

Downtown's renaissance has been aided since 1975 by the Centre City Development Corporation, a seven-member non-profit redevelopment agency, the first of its kind in California.

The Bank of Commerce once housed an oyster bar favored by Sheriff Wyatt Earp.

The new Downtown: at the Hahn Company developed 140 million dollar Horton Plaza, crowds gather around the historic Jessops Clock which has long been a San Diego landmark. The hand-tiled Plazzo Tower is right.

Questions: There are those who wonder if they will have a place in San Diego's future. Along the embarcadero, captains of the tuna clippers debate how long they will be able to use San Diego as home port. In June, 1984, the Van Camp Sea Food cannery closed down. The following October, San Pedro's Star-Kist plant stopped canning tuna. To deliver their catch, the big clippers must make the long voyage to canneries in American Samoa. Each voyage can consume as much as $70,000 in fuel. The downtown rebirth is a mixed blessing, or no blessing at all, for the urban poor. As increasing numbers of the middle class return to the "Urban Frontier," rents and prices go up. Gentrification has caused a sad reverse migration as the poor are displaced with constantly diminishing housing alternatives. Horton House, Columbia Tower, and Lions Manor are downtown low-cost apartment houses built to ease some of the pain of urban renewal.

In San Diego's inland valleys, farmers worry about water. The going price for water in the Imperial Valley is $9.50 per acre-foot. In the county's Ramona Water District, a farmer may pay up to $450 an acre-foot. Farmers with greenhouses can face $40,000 a year in gas and electric bills. The total acreage in San Diego County farmland continues to shrink. From 1978 to 1983, farming ceased on 10,000 acres. The county once boasted 8,000 acres of vineyards. Today, only about 1,000 remain. Like the tuna captains, San Diego's farmers can only wonder how long they can hold out.

The border entry at San Ysidro is one of the busiest in the world with over 32 million crossings in 1984. In January, 1985, a second entryway was opened on Otay Mesa a few miles to the east to help relieve the pressure.

For San Diego's minorities, the concern is about future jobs. Increasingly, new industries are locating on the mesas north of Mission Valley. South of Highway 8, which cuts down the length of Mission Valley, the only promise of new jobs seems to be in downtown's redevelopment. And the competition for those jobs will be keen.

The Rev. George Walker Smith, one of the black community's most eloquent spokesmen, speaks of the frustration among many of San Diego's poor minorities: "San Diego basically is developing more and more into two separate but inequal societies . . . It is unfortunate that our civic and political leaders seem to be insensitive, if not completely indifferent, to what's happening."

Unlike old soldiers, old sailors don't fade away. They move to San Diego. There are more retired admirals in Coronado than any other city in the world.

One enduring source of jobs is the Navy: two major training bases in the city, the Naval Training Center and the Marine Corps Recruit Depot; naval air stations at North Island and Miramar; the naval hospital at Balboa Park; and the huge 32nd Street base, the Submarine Base at Point Loma, and the amphibious warfare base at Coronado. Over 100 ships call San Diego their home port, and over 100,000 uniformed personnel are stationed throughout the county. In 1983, military personnel and their families made up about six percent of San Diego County's 2.06 million population and pumped an estimated $4.75 billion into the county's gross regional product.

A Short History of San Diego

There is occasional friction between the military and San Diego's civilian citizens. When construction began on the new naval hospital buildings in Balboa Park's Florida Canyon in 1983, conservationists protested to little avail. In January, 1985, during a naval exercise, thin silvery strips tossed in the wind to foil radar accidently blew inland. When the strips landed on utility lines, massive power outages resulted. But the navy remains a vital part of San Diego's economy, and communication between the military and the city's leaders is frequent and open.

Tourism: "The only things to do in San Diego," Jim Murray once grumped in his Los Angeles *Times* sports column, "are join the Navy or go to the Zoo." The Navy is still very much a part of San Diego and so is the Zoo, but today's visitor will find numerous other attractions, each of which provide a solid source of employment for San Diegans.

One of the most popular places in San Diego with tourists and locals alike is Mission Bay's Sea World. When the marine park first opened in 1964, it was

Fading Scene: As competition increases for land and water, farm workers, like these strawberry planters, are becoming a less familiar San Diego sight.

Reborn: Once sadly neglected, the Horton Grand Hotel was restored to its Victorian splendor and reopened in 1986.

In 1984, Old Town State Historic Park remained the tourist favorite with over three million visitors. Sea World, with a rise in attendance to 2,708,000, pulled into second place ahead of the Zoo (which reported 2,664,000). Coming in fourth was Cabrillo National Monument, with 1,306,424 visitors.

small (22 acres) and quietly modest, offering two shows and a single salt water aquarium. Over the years, it has increased five-fold and now boasts six shows, four aquariums, and 30 exhibits. Killer whales flash through the waters of a 1.25 million-gallon whale facility, while nearby some of the largest sharks in captivity swim lazy circles in a 400,000-gallon aquarium. In the new Penguin Encounter, the world's largest collection of penguins cavort happily in 5,000 square feet of chilly Antarctic environment.

The newest major attraction in San Diego is the 14-acre Seaport Village on the Embarcadero. Located a few blocks south of the Broadway Pier, the $18 million Village is a collection of theme shops and restaurants. Complementing it nearby is the Embarcadero Marina Park with lawns, shade trees, bicycling and jogging paths, and fishing areas. Since its opening in 1980, Seaport Village has become popular with residents and visitors alike.

San Diego Bay, once crowded with warships, is now crowded with plea-sure boats. In addition to the familiar harbor excursion boats, afternoon sailors can choose among two miniature Mississippi-style riverboats, a 1905 sailing yacht, and a 220-passenger hydrofoil. The mid-1980s has seen the return of large cruise ships to San Diego for the first time in a half-century. And today's liners, like the 20,000-ton *Pacific Princess* (made famous by the "Love Boat" television series), dwarf the small coastal liners that visited San Diego in the

1930s. In addition to the *Pacific Princess*, several other cruise ships include San Diego in their itineraries: the 17,000-ton luxury liner *Daphne*, the American Hawaii liners *Constitution* and *Independence* (the only large ocean-going liners under an American flag) and the Holland America flagship *Rotterdam*.

Amid the modern hotels and gleaming liners, San Diego's past has not been forgotten. Old Town is enjoying a brisk renaissance of its own. In the closing months of 1984, three replicas of vanished historical buildings were under construction. They were the U.S. House (a former boarding house), the Light-Freeman building (owned in the 1830s by San Diego's first black merchants) and the Thomas Wrightington residence. These three buildings are only the first to be reconstructed as part of Old Town State Historic Park; eventually there will be seven.

The next few years will see even more ambitious plans become reality. A 600,000-square foot convention center will open its doors in the fall of 1987 on the edge of San Diego Bay. The 25,000 hotel rooms available in 1984 will be increased in number as several planned hotels are completed and older hotels are refurbished and expanded. Once a virtual cottage industry, tourism in San Diego has become big business, a business with an almost unlimited future.

Killer Whale: Shamu is a leading attraction at Seaworld, the city's leading tourist attraction. Each year San Diego's 20 million visitors spend more than $1 billion, and provide 70,000 jobs.

Hopes and Concerns: San Diego, blessed by nature and optimism in high California style, faces a future filled with promise. But there are concerns that must be faced. The ever-increasing population brings with it new pressures. Smog, once a curiosity, has become too common. The number of homeless downtown grows as the destitute come to find warmth in the sun. The San Diego Rescue Mission, which has fed (without government aid) 225 million people since 1955, reports that the average transient now is only 27 and seems to grow younger each year. And not all of those displaced by urban renewal have found new homes.

Water will become a greater problem in the coming years. Sometimes there will not be enough. In 1963, *San Diego Magazine* noted, "If everyone entitled to water from the Colorado River took his full share, we would be rationing the stuff in San Diego right now." As Arizona takes its share, water rationing may well become a fact of life in San Diego.

Occasionally, briefly, there can be too much water. During wet years, the San Diego River creeps perilously close to Mission Valley office buildings and shoppping centers. South of San Diego, the murky Tia Juana River winds into the United States from Mexico, bringing with it millions of gallons of sewage. In especially rainy years, it can swell to dangerous proportions. In early 1980, it rampaged through the rich farmland of the Tia Juana River Valley on the

In 1984, Mayor Roger Hedgecock was indicted on charges of perjury and conspiracy in the wake of the J. Dominelli collapse. He joins other San Diego figures brushed by scandal, including ex-mayor Frank Curran, indicted in 1970, and one-time "Mr. San Diego" C. Arnholt Smith, sentenced to prison in 1984.

Timeless: Mission San Diego's bells still ring as a reminder of the modern city's proud Spanish heritage.

American side of the border. Houses were torn in half, farms flooded, and bridges washed away.

Amid the shining towers of a new downtown, some of the small things that give a city its character have been lost. Baggy pants comedian "Hello There" Eddie Ware no longer entertains sailors at the Hollywood Burlesk. One no longer sees printers on Broadway, with their square paper hats come up from the *Union-Tribune* presses for a breath of air. The *Union-Tribune* presses are in Mission Valley now and the Hollywood Burlesk Theater has been torn down and carted away. The "nickle snatcher" boats no longer chug back and forth across the bay between North Island and the foot of Broadway; the bridge does their work now.

San Diego is a city whose people do not easily move away. Job seekers readily accept lower pay rather than look where the competition is less fierce. Planners wonder when the city's resources will be taxed to the limit; but new arrivals still come in their thousands each year.

They come to where, on Sunday afternoons, hundreds of sails, brilliant white against the water, pattern the bay. Where the patina of the past is comfortable against the harsher glint of the present. In the bustling downtown, there is still time for a quiet lunch in the sun.

"San Diego . . . bustling, brawny—downright chic."
—U.S. News and World Report, November, 1982

Finishing Touches: Sand castles are anything but child's play as the G.O.P.P.I.T.S. (Group of People Playing in the Sand) Club completes their entry in Imperial Beach's U.S. Open Sand Castle Competition. Each year the July event draws over 100,000 spectators.

Selected Bibliography

Benchley, Belle. *My Life in a Man-Made Jungle*. Boston: Little, Brown & Co., 1940. Pleasant, chatty book capturing the flavor of the 1930s San Diego Zoo.

Bruns, Bill. *A World of Animals: The San Diego Zoo and the Wild Animal Park*. New York: Harry N. Abrams, 1983. Complete, well done, for all who love animals. Beautifully illustrated by photographer Ron Garrison.

Dutton, Davis (editor). *San Diego and the Back Country*. New York: Ballatine Books, 1972.

Ellsberg, Helen. *Mines of Julian*. Glendale, California: La Siesta Press, 1972. Only 72 pages but the best treatment of San Diego's gold country I've come across.

Friends of the UCSD Library. *San Diego, California: A Bicentennial Bibliography. 1769-1969*, San Diego: University of California at San Diego, 1969.

Greenwalt, Emmett. *The Point Loma Community in California, 1897-1942*. Berkeley: University of California Press, 1955. The strange and wonderful world that was Lomaland.

Miller, Max. *I Cover the Waterfront*. New York: Ballantine Books, 1971. Reprint of 1932 book which in turn was reprint of Miller's *San Diego Sun* newspaper columns.

MacMullen, Jerry. *They Came by Sea: A Pictorial History of San Diego Bay*. San Diego: Ward Ritchie Press and the Maritime Museum Association of San Diego, 1969. Before his 1981 death, MacMullen was the dean of San Diego maritime historians.

MacMullen, Jerry. *They Came by Sea: A Pictorial History of San Diego Bay*. San Diego: Ward Ritchie Press and the Maritime Museum Association of San Diego, 1969. Before his 1981 death, MacMullen was the dean of San Diego maritime historians.

MacPhail, Elizabeth. *The Story of New San Diego and of its Founder Alonzo E. Horton*. San Diego: San Diego Historical Society, 1979.

Morgan, Neil. *San Diego: The Unconventional City*. San Diego: Morgan House, 1972.

Peet, Mary Rockwood. *San Pasqual: A Crack in the Hills*. Ramona, California: Ballena Press, 1972. Includes a well done chapter on the Battle of San Pasqual.

Shannon, Don. *Mission to Metropolis: A History of San Diego*. National City, California: Bayport Press, 1981. Pocket book-sized, sharply etched and fast moving.

Wegeforth, Harry. *It Began With a Roar*. San Diego: San Diego Zoological Society. Rambling at times, but when you put the book down, you feel as if you've just spent a pleasant evening listening to "Dr. Harry" talk about the Zoo.

The late Richard Pourade's seven-volume history of San Diego published in the 1960s by Copley Books are by far the most extensive and well documented books on the subject. For any local historian, it is difficult if not impossible to find material where Pourade has not been first.

PICTURE CREDITS

Courtesy, The Bancroft Library: 6, 8, 12, 25, 28, 30, 33, 40, 45, 53, 55, 67, 69, 77, 90, 113, 115, 118, 120.

San Diego Historical Society —Ticor Collection: 10, 15, 20, 23, 31, 34, 37, 44, 46, 50, 56, 58, 61, 62, 66, 68, 71, 74, 78, 79, 82, 83, 88, 91, 93, 95, 110, 114.

Zoological Society of San Diego: 96, 99, 100, 101, 102, 103, 104, 105, 106, 107, 108, 109.

San Diego Museum of Man: 9.

Lowie Museum of Anthropology, University of California, Berkeley: 17.

San Diego Convention and Visitors Bureau: 18, 126, 134.

Centre City Development Corp.: 129.

Sea World: 133.

D. Schaferkotter: 135.

Horton Grand Hotel/Wise Communications: 132.

The Hahn Company: 129.

Index

Note: Page numbers in italics refer to photographs and maps.